A-Z of Challenging Behaviour Series

A FOR ARGUMENTATIVE BEHAVIOUR

Dolly Bhargava

Master of Special Education

Copyright © 2020 Behaviour Help Pty Ltd. The contents of this guide (text and graphics) are protected by international copyright law. No part of this publication may be reproduced, stored in a retrieval system, transmitted, broadcast or communicated in any form or by any means, optical, digital, electronic, mechanical, photocopying, recording or otherwise, without written permission of Behaviour Help. To obtain permission, email: admin@behaviourhelp.com

Behaviour data collection forms can be reproduced with citation: Bhargava, D. (2020). <u>A for Argumentative: Positive Behaviour Support.</u> Melbourne, Vic: Behaviour Help Pty Ltd.

Please note the word 'child' in this guide refers to children of all ages (toddler, preschooler, primary and high school). The information set out in this guide is of a general nature only and not exhaustive on the subject matter. You should consider whether the information is appropriate to the needs of the child you support and your circumstances. This guide should not be used as a diagnostic tool. When implementing any recommendations contained in this guide, exercise independent skill and judgement. If you have any concerns about your child's behaviours, please discuss them with a doctor who can provide guidance and/or a referral to the relevant professional.

A - Z of Challenging Behaviours Series

Titles

A for Argumentative

A for Attention-Seeking

B for Biting

C for Cheating

D for Defiance

E for Excessive Reassurance Seeking

E for Excessive Technology Use

F for Flopping

H for Hitting

I for Impulsivity

K for Kicking

L for Lying

R for Repetitive Questioning

S for School Refusal Behaviour

S for Separation Anxiety

S for Stealing

T for Task Avoidance

The list of titles is being expanded all the time. For the latest, please refer to www.behaviourhelp.com

ACKNOWLEDGEMENTS

I wish to thank the following people for helping me put this series together despite COVID-19 restrictions.

My husband and children – Gaj, Navina and Ethan
My beyond amazing editor - Keith Ougden

TABLE OF CONTENTS

1. PREFACE 1
2. INTRODUCTION TO ARGUMENTATIVE BEHAVIOUR 3
3. DEFINING POSITIVE BEHAVIOUR SUPPORT 7
4. ASSESS-MANAGE-PREVENT STAGES 10
5. ASSESS STAGE 13
6. MANAGE STAGE 42
7. PREVENT STAGE 65
8. CONCLUSION 82
9. REFERENCES 83
10. APPENDIX: BEHAVIOUR HELP WEB-BASED APP 85
11. ABOUT THE AUTHOR 87

1. PREFACE

All children experience difficulties with managing their emotions and behaviours at one time or another. With understanding, support and encouragement, most children learn the skills they need to manage this. However, some children repeatedly engage in emotional and behavioural responses that can cause serious harm to others and/or themselves. Despite best efforts and intentions, the child has difficulties learning how to manage their emotions and behaviours and the situation does not appear to improve.

As a parent, caregiver educator, support staff or professional, facing the child's challenging emotional and behavioural responses daily can result in feeling stressed, exhausted and disheartened. If any of this sounds familiar, then this guide will provide a roadmap developed from the evidenced-based approach of Positive Behaviour Support (PBS) to help guide the child to learn positive ways of behaving and managing their emotions in a variety of contexts (e.g. childcare, early childhood, primary and secondary school, disability and youth services).

A for Argumentative provides a description of argumentative behaviour, and then introduces the Positive Behaviour Support (PBS) approach. This guide includes many detailed and practical ideas to develop a comprehensive PBS plan by guiding the reader through the three distinct stages of PBS:

- ASSESS: How to identify the reasons for the argumentative behaviour,
- MANAGE: How to respond when argumentative behaviour occurs, and
- PREVENT: How to minimise or eliminate the occurrence of argumentative behaviour.

The guide contains practical tools (forms, checklists and strategies) to assist the process; the forms are available as a free download in the *Free Resources* section of www.behaviourhelp.com. The website also includes access to the web-based Behaviour Help app www.behaviourhelp.com/app/#/ signup. The app contains the can be used to systematically assess incidents of challenging behaviour and develop individualised behaviour management and prevention plans.

Please remember, it is never too late to change a behaviour. Change does not happen overnight; instead, it is a process that takes time. Change is also not a straightforward process. Instead it is like a rollercoaster where there are ups and downs, moves forward, moves backwards and then forward again. The key is that with persistence, patience, and perseverance the child can gradually learn positive ways of behaving and managing their emotions.

I would like to take this opportunity to commend you for taking a step in this journey to make a difference and create a better future for your child.

Best wishes,
Dolly Bhargava

2. INTRODUCTION TO ARGUMENTATIVE BEHAVIOUR

Arguing in all relationships is normal. It is impossible for two or more people to agree on everything all the time, disagreements will happen from time to time. Disagreements can be caused by differences in: views, opinions, beliefs, ideas, priorities and motivations, ways things are organised, carried out and completed, misunderstandings in communication, misinterpretations of expectations, and resistance to change and doing things differently, unreleased fear, anger and frustration.

When there is a disagreement, argumentation is the dialogic process in which two or more people engage in a debate of opposing claims (Kuhn & Udell, 2007). This exchange allows one to state their needs, concerns and views which creates the opportunity for the other person/s to become aware of what is causing the upset and for everyone involved to address the cause and move forward past the argument.

Children develop this critical lifelong skill on how to construct and handle arguments as they mature and through guidance from adults in their environment.

There are healthy and unhealthy ways of exchanging and addressing disagreements.

The example below shows a healthy way of exchanging and addressing a disagreement:

Jane is in year 9. She is sitting at the back of the classroom on one of the bean bags looking at her laptop. Her teacher starts to give instructions to the class informing them they need to break into groups, find a spot to sit and answer the worksheet questions. Jane is distracted as she wants to finish writing an email. She soon realises she doesn't know what to do so she leaves the laptop on the bean bag and walks up to the teacher to find out what she needs to do. A group of girls who are looking for a spot to sit, see the laptop on the bean bag. They do not know whose laptop it is and think someone has just accidentally left the laptop there. So, they put it on a nearby table and sit on the beanbag. Jane returns and starts to feel herself getting a bit panicked. She takes a deep breath to calm herself down says, 'Excuse me! Have you seen my laptop?' The girls point to where it is and explain why they put it there. Jane responds by saying, 'That makes sense but I am sorry, but I was sitting on the beanbag with my laptop. I would like to keep working here, are you able to find another spot.' The girls say 'Jane, do you mind if we keep sitting here because all the other spots for big groups are taken. There is a single couch on the other side of the room with a power point that you can use to charge your laptop.' Jane has a think, understands their viewpoint and says, 'Sure' and walks away.

The example below shows an unhealthy way of exchanging and addressing a disagreement:

Flora is in year 9. She is sitting at the back of the classroom on one of the bean bags looking at her laptop. Her teacher starts to give instructions to the class informing them they need to break into groups, find a spot to sit and answer the worksheet questions. Flora is distracted as she wants to finish writing an email. She soon realises she doesn't know what to do so she leaves the laptop on the bean bag and walks up to the teacher to find out what she needs to do. A group of girls who are looking for a spot, see the laptop on the bean bag. They do not know whose laptop it is and thinking someone has just accidentally left the laptop there they put it on a nearby table and sit on the bean bag. Flora returns and when she sees the girls sitting on the bean bag she can feel her face and body getting hot. She is consumed by instantaneous overwhelming rage at the group of girls.

She doesn't know how to control her emotions and calm herself down and instead yells at the girls, 'What are you doing here? I was sitting here. Where's my laptop? Did you steal it?' The girls say, 'Flora, we didn't know you were sitting here. Your name isn't on the bean bag and your dumb laptop is over there.' Flora rolls her eyes, interrupts them and starts swearing at them and threatens them by saying, 'You better get up now or I am going to throw your laptop in the bin.' The teacher, hearing the commotion, comes over. The girls explain to the teacher what is happening. The teacher says to Flora, 'The girls do have a good point. Why don't you go and sit on the couch?' The teacher then reaches out to gently touch Flora on her arm. The teacher's words and actions appear to make the situation worse. Flora starts screaming at the top of her voice, 'Don't touch me! You always listen to everyone else. You don't care about what I want!' Flora starts to kick the girls. The teacher quickly intervenes and asks the girls to move. The girls stand up and leave. Flora smirks, grabs her laptop and sits on her bean bag.

Argumentative behaviour becomes a concern when the following occur:

- the frequency (i.e. how often a child exhibits argumentative behaviour) becomes excessive
- the duration (i.e. how long each incident of the argumentative behaviour lasts) becomes excessive
- the intensity (i.e. the strength of the argumentative behaviour) escalates from minor behaviours into extreme behaviours
- the argumentative behaviour negatively impacts the child's participation in activities, interaction with others, their day-to-day functioning and development.

It is important to note that argumentative behaviour exists for a variety of reasons, and is particularly prominent in children with depression, anxiety, Oppositional defiant disorder, Conduct disorder, Intermittent explosive disorder and Attention deficit hyperactivity disorder.

Supporting an argumentative child is exhausting. It is as if you are walking on eggshells because you do not know what is going to upset them, and every demand you place on them results in an argument. For example, what may seem to a be a simple instruction such as 'sit on the mat' or 'join a group activity' may result in a straight out 'No', and if the adult does not back down a heated argument results. Adults also become wary about confronting the child because the child sees themselves as definitely right and others definitely wrong, which means that it is hard to reason with the child or back down. It can leave everyone feeling at a loss because nobody knows how to set limits and get the child to do what they are supposed to be doing.

Below are some examples:

John has been diagnosed with Oppositional defiant disorder. John wants a pen from the table where Paul is sitting. As Paul is in the way, John walks up to him and pushes him so he can get the pen. Paul, who fell off his chair when John pushed him, starts crying. The teacher comes over and tells John to apologise, but John looks confused and says, 'Why do I need to apologise? If anyone should be apologising, it's him.' Stunned, the teacher asks why Paul needs to apologise. John says, 'I wanted the pen off the table. Paul saw me coming. He should have moved out of the way. But because he was in my way, he left me no option. I had to move him. I didn't even push him as hard as he says, it was just a tap. He's being a drama queen and just likes to whinge. He should apologise for being in my way.'

Harry and his friend Timothy are caught running in the hallway during recess. The teacher who catches them says, 'You know you shouldn't be in here. Go outside.' Harry, who has Conduct disorder, starts to swear and argue with the teacher. For everything she says, he has something to say. He has to have the final word. When the teacher realises that the situation is going to escalate, she tells the students to go outside; she returns to the staff room. Harry thinks he's won. Now, whenever Harry sees that teacher, he smiles at her and swears just loud enough for her to hear.

When a child begins to persistently exhibit argumentative behaviour, the climate of the context (e.g. childcare, early childhood, primary and secondary school, disability support and youth services) can change dramatically. A considerable amount of time and energy can be spent on the child showing the argumentative behaviour, which can have a deleterious effect on the quality of the learning experience for all the children. Research consistently shows that managing behaviour is linked to staff experiencing high levels of stress, burnout and job dissatisfaction.

Hence, argumentative behaviour affects everyone involved and the child who is exhibiting argumentative behaviour requires necessary help to learn positive ways of behaving and managing their emotions.

3. DEFINING POSITIVE BEHAVIOUR SUPPORT

Positive Behaviour Support (PBS) is an evidence-based approach that is used to eliminate or minimise the occurrence of challenging behaviours. "Challenging behaviour is any behaviour that interferes with children's learning, development, success at play; is harmful to the child, other children or adults; and puts them at high risk for later social problems or school failure" (Klass, Guskin & Thomas, 1995, p. 5). Examples of challenging behaviours include aggressive behaviours, destructive behaviours, inappropriate social behaviours, self-injurious and withdrawn behaviours. In this guide, argumentative behaviour will be addressed by utilising the PBS approach to enhance the child's communication and social, emotional, behavioural and learning outcomes.

Argumentative behaviour is like the tip of the iceberg. It is important to look beneath the surface to work out why the child is exhibiting the argumentative behaviour.

PBS recognises that there is no single cause for argumentative behaviour. It is a complex behaviour that is a product of the interaction between multiple factors contributing to its development and persistence, as explained by the bio-psycho-social model. This model considers how different biological, psychological and social factors interact and combine to influence behaviour:

- Biological factors include the child's age, gender, neurobiology, physiology and genetics (Schick, & Cierpka, 2016).
- Psychological factors include the child's cognition, emotion, self-esteem, behaviour, coping and social information processing skills (Reisinger, 2014).
- Social/environmental factors include parenting and family factors, educational environment factors; social environmental factors and community factors (Griffiths & Gardner, 2002; Meysamie et al., 2013).

To help identify and address these factors it is important to access various professionals:

health (e.g. General practitioner/doctor, paediatrician), mental health (e.g. psychiatrist, psychologist and counsellor), allied health (e.g. occupational therapist, speech pathologist, physiotherapist) and educational (e.g. learning specialists).

In this guide strategies to address argumentative behaviour within the childcare, preschool, kindergarten, primary and secondary school, disability support and youth services context, will be addressed by utilising the PBS approach. Whilst in these contexts it is not possible to control all the factors that contribute to the argumentative behaviour outside of its context, by collaboratively working in partnership with parents, caregivers and professionals, factors specific to the context can be addressed to help the child achieve better communication, social, emotional, behavioural and learning outcomes.

Argumentative behaviour does not occur in a vacuum, but within a context. There are three main context-related factors that impact the child and their behaviour: the environment, the activity and the interaction. These factors place different demands on the child and when any of these demands outweigh the child's skills to cope with them, the child engages in argumentative behaviour. Being argumentative may be the only way the child has learnt how to respond to these demands and get their message across.

Example: Ben was playing on his iPad. When the timer rang his teacher asked him to put the iPad away. Ben said, 'No.' The teacher asked him again to which he replied, 'Why?' the teacher explained that he needs to get the rest of his maths work done. Ben said, 'I don't want to do the rest of the work.' His teacher reminded him that was the rule. The argument went on for a while and after the hundredth time of Ben asking 'Why?', in exasperation the teacher said, 'Because I said so.' This triggered Ben and he screamed, 'You are not the boss of me. You can't make me!'

Some of the skills needed to cope with this interaction include:

- Healthy ways of arguing – Does Ben know how to express his needs in a respectful manner? Can Ben think flexibly to allow himself to see the situation in alternative ways? Does he know how to negotiate with his teacher to identify a mutually agreeable situation?
- Transition skills – Can Ben transition from a highly preferred activity to a highly non-preferred activity without any additional supports? Is

the timer with no countdown reminders (e.g. 5 minutes to go, 4 minutes to go, 3 minutes to go) a sufficient prewarning for Ben?

- Emotional regulation – Can Ben regulate his emotions and stay calm?
- Compliance skills – Can Ben comply with instructions where power is used to coerce him to do something?
- Communication skills – Can Ben explain to his teacher that he is playing a game that has levels and he needs to finish the level? Can Ben negotiate with his teacher that he finishes the level and then he can do the work?
- Learning skills – Can Ben do the Maths work?

As Ben does not have the skills needed to cope, he resorts to arguing with his teacher.

The examples highlight that argumentative behaviour is not without purpose. It is never too late to address argumentative behaviour, even if it has been occurring for a while.

PBS provides a road map to address argumentative behaviour by using a holistic approach to develop a comprehensive and individualised PBS plan in three stages: Assess-Manage-Prevent.

4. ASSESS-MANAGE-PREVENT STAGES

PBS involves three stages:

- The Assess stage aims to identify the triggers (events) that contribute to the occurrence of the argumentative behaviour and understand the purpose (function) of the argumentative behaviour. These findings will inform the development of a comprehensive and individualised PBS intervention plan that is based on information gathered from the Manage and Prevent stages.
- The Manage stage aims to provide guidelines to help everyone supporting the child to respond to the argumentative behaviour in a planned, safe, and least disruptive manner.
- The Prevent stage aims to prevent the occurrence of the argumentative behaviours by minimising or avoiding the triggers that cause the argumentative behaviour by tailoring the activity, environment, and interactions. The Prevent stage also aims to teach the child positive ways of communicating their messages and managing their emotions and behaviours.
- Once the PBS plan is implemented it is important to evaluate the effectiveness of the Manage and Prevent stages by repeating the Assess stage to measure the amount or type of progress that has been made. This can help you determine the effectiveness of the Manage and Prevent strategies and refine and adapt them to ultimately help the child reach their full potential.

'Unity is strength ... when there is teamwork and collaboration, wonderful things can be achieved'.

– Mattie Stepanek

Dealing with a child's argumentative behaviour can be extremely stressful, demoralising and disheartening. It is also unlikely that any one person will have all the answers to the challenges. Along with the parents and caregivers, it is useful to identify a team of people who know the child well. This could include educators, administration staff, professionals, disability support and community staff who can work together for the benefit of the child.

Each person on the team has their special knowledge and perspective. By working in partnership through each stage in a unified way, they can help the child learn positive ways of behaving and managing their emotions.

Depending on the child's needs, identify all the people who will be involved in the team. Use the *Team Member Chart* provided on the next page to record the names, roles, and contexts in which they support the child.

Team Member Chart

Child name _____

Recorder name _____

Date _____

Team member name	Role	Context where they support the child (e.g. home, day centre, school and therapy)

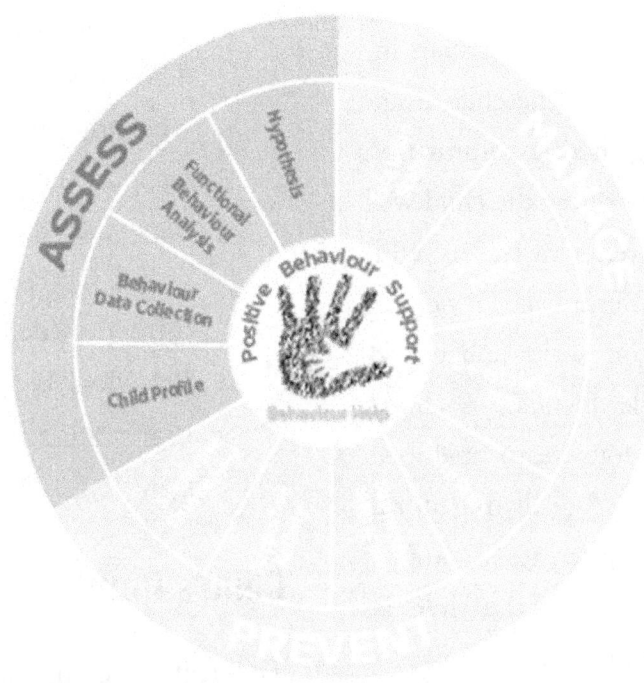

5. ASSESS STAGE

Assessment is the process of understanding the reasons, purpose or function of the argumentative behaviour.

The Assess stage helps to identity:

- Activities during which the argumentative behaviour occurs,
- Environments in which the argumentative behaviour occurs, and
- People dealing with the argumentative behaviour.

Once the circumstances in which the argumentative behaviour occurs are identified, the triggers (events) that contribute to the occurrence of the child's argumentative behaviour can be investigated. To carry out the assessment, a combination of indirect and direct assessment methods is used.

The Assess stage involves the team working through the checklist tasks listed:

Assess Stage Checklist:

- Child's profile – Indirect methods include interviews with the child if appropriate and gathering information from people who know the child well such as their parents, caregivers, educators and professionals, reviewing any reports, rating scales and checklists. This guide includes a child's profile that various team members can contribute to. By collating all the information, it will create a comprehensive picture of who the child is, their abilities and needs.
- Behaviour data collection forms – This is a direct method and includes observing a child during real time and measuring the argumentative behaviour. Measurable dimensions include frequency (how often it occurs), duration (how long it can last) and intensity (how severe it is). The forms can be used to collate the data over the course of at least a few weeks or longer. Collecting data can help identify and understand any patterns of behaviour.
- Functional Behaviour Analysis (FBA) – This is a direct method that involves reflecting on an incident by answering a series of questions to identify what happened before and after the argumentative behaviour. These results can be used to work out what triggered the argumentative behaviour and the purpose (function) that the argumentative behaviour served. To complete an FBA, use the form provided in this guide or the Behaviour Help web-based app (www.behaviourhelp.com/app/#/signup).

Child's Profile

To create a comprehensive picture of the child, their abilities and needs the following areas need to be considered. If the child has difficulties in any of these areas, intervention is critical. Without the appropriate supports, services and strategies these unaddressed difficulties can contribute to the child exhibiting argumentative behaviour.

General health

Health is a state of physical, mental and social well-being that allows the child to adequately cope with demands of daily life. It is important to investigate any health-related issues (e.g. illness, infections, allergies and pain) first, particularly if the behaviour has suddenly become more intense and/or is not responding to trialled behaviour management strategies.

It is also important to record any diagnosis the child has. Diagnosis of conditions describe a broad range of health conditions including:

- Chronic illnesses (e.g. cancer, diabetes and asthma),
- Mental health conditions (e.g. anxiety, depression and schizophrenia),
- Trauma and stress related disorders
- Neurodevelopmental disorders (e.g. autism spectrum disorder, intellectual disability, attention deficit hyperactivity disorder and Down syndrome), communication disorders (e.g. language disorder, stuttering and social/language disorder), motor disorders (e.g. Tourette's disorder, dyspraxia and tic disorder),
- Feeding and eating disorders (e.g. anorexia nervosa, bulimia nervosa or binge eating disorder),
- Elimination disorder (e.g. encopresis, enuresis),
- Sleep-wake disorders (e.g. obstructive sleep apnoea, parasomnias, narcolepsy, and restless leg syndrome),
- Personality disorders (e.g. bipolar personality disorder),
- Substance-related and addictive disorders, and
- Disruptive, impulse-control and conduct disorders (e.g. oppositional defiant disorder, conduct disorder, intermittent explosive disorder, kleptomania and pyromania).

Every child is unique and even children with the same diagnosis will have different abilities, needs and preferences. When completing the profile, it is important to record the impact of the diagnosis on the child's skill development. This will help identify the necessary supports, strategies and services the child needs to reach their full potential.

Information on any medications, alcohol or drugs the child may be consuming needs to be recorded. Any side effects that affect the child's learning (e.g. memory issues), emotions (e.g. irritability), behaviour (e.g. overreaction) and communication need to be understood. Intervention is critical for addressing the child's health needs.

Visual skills

Vision plays an important role in a child's growth, development and daily performance. Disease, damage or injury to any part of the visual system (i.e. eye, visual pathway to the brain or visual centre of the brain) causes a vision impairment which results in reduced visual functioning for their social, psychological, communication, physical and academic performance (Department of Education, 2011; Rainey et. al, 2016). Intervention is critical for helping the child develop vision skills.

Hearing skills

Hearing plays an important role in the development of speech and language skills, social interaction skills and daily performance. Hearing impairment or loss occurs when there is a problem with or damage to one or more parts of the hearing mechanism (i.e. one or more parts of the ear or ears, hearing pathway to the brain or the hearing centre of the brain) (Department of Education, 2011). Hearing impairment can impose basic limitations on a child, in terms of access to spoken language, access to environmental auditory experiences and ease of interacting with a wide range of people. Intervention is critical for helping the child develop listening skills.

Physical skills

Physical skills are comprised of gross motor skills (e.g. sit, stand and walk) and/or fine motor skills (e.g. eat, write and cut). Gross motor and fine motor skills allow a child to explore and interact with the world around them. When a child has difficulties with these skill sets, it can negatively impact their ability to move or coordinate and control their bodies to perform the skills necessary for accessing, participating in and learning from their environment. These difficulties can lead to learning difficulties, low self-esteem and frustration. Intervention is critical for helping the child develop physical skills.

Sensory needs

There are eight types of sensory information that are received by different parts of the body: vision (eyes), auditory/hearing (ears), olfactory/smell (nose), tory/taste (tongue), vestibular/balance and movement (inner ears), tactile/touch (skin), proprioception/pressure and body awareness (joints and tendons) and interoception/messages from inside the body (internal organs).

Sensory processing refers to the way the brain receives, processes and organises the information received through the senses and turns them into appropriate motor and behavioural responses. Some children have a Sensory Processing Disorder (SPD). SPD is a neurological condition that means the nervous system is not able to process and organise the messages received from the senses into appropriate responses.

Children with SPD may show hypersensitivity, where they react too strongly to the sensory information, or hyposensitivity, where they are seemingly unaware of the input. If a child is hyposensitive, they will crave or seek sensory input to keep their bodies calm. If a child is hypersensitive, they will react too strongly to the sensory information.

To address the child's sensory needs, they need a 'sensory diet' designed by an Occupational Therapist. A 'sensory diet' is a carefully designed, personalised activity plan that provides the right combination of sensory input a child needs to stay alert, engaged, focused and organised throughout the day. Each day depending on the child's needs a sensory diet is created to provide the necessary combinations of sensory input to 'feed or nourish' the child's nervous system at frequent intervals throughout the day to help the child stay regulated (Prizant et al., 2006). Without a sensory diet the child may not receive the necessary sensory input throughout the day, become dysregulated and exhibit argumentative behaviours to seek or avoid sensory input. Intervention is critical for addressing the child's sensory needs.

Sleep patterns

Persistent poor sleep quality or not enough sleep results in difficulties with attention, memory, reasoning and problem solving and lowers the child's ability to control their emotions and behaviours. Research has shown the link between persistent sleeping difficulties and an increase in negative moods and challenging behaviours. Intervention is critical for addressing the child's sleep needs.

Eating and drinking skills

If a child is a picky eater and doesn't eat because they don't like the taste, temperature, colour or texture of what is being offered or is not getting enough food and water, they will often be feeling hungry or thirsty. The feeling of hunger or thirst can make a child go into the fight/flight/fright mode which lowers the child's ability to control their impulses, emotions and behaviours. Intervention is critical for addressing the child's eating and/or drinking skills.

Communication skills

Communication is a two-way process involving an exchange and flow of information and ideas between no fewer than two people. Some children have difficulty with understanding and expressing their ideas. For example, Genevieve often misinterprets situations. She will begin arguing with someone even though it does not involve her. She also has difficulties with clearly, succinctly and in an orderly manner explaining the reasons to support her argument. Her speech often conveys a sense of incoherence which causes the other person to make fun of her for not making any sense resulting in escalation of the situation. Intervention is critical for addressing the child's communication skills.

Emotional regulation skills

Emotional regulation is the ability to identify, express and manage emotions in healthy ways. A child may have difficulty with identifying and expressing their emotions which causes frustration. The child may not know how to manage their emotions and use challenging behaviours to express their emotions. Some children become overwhelmed by feelings, whether positive (e.g. happy, overexcited or proud) or negative (e.g. angry, hungry, tired, frustrated, fearful, stressed or disappointed). Consequently, the brain gets flooded by the emotion, which lowers the brain's ability to think and act rationally. This results in the child being unable to control their behaviour. For example, after an argument with the teacher, Lennox will go under the table and bang as hard as he can with his hands, feet or head to make the table move and make it difficult or impossible for other children to sit and do activities. He tries to make as much noise as possible, which results in the room being difficult to be in and the activities disrupted or broken. Intervention is critical for addressing the child's emotional regulation skills.

Social skills

Social skills are the non-verbal and verbal communication skills used to interact with others, according to the social conventions of a particular context. Non-verbal communication skills include body language, facial expressions, posture, proximity, listening, grooming and hygiene. Verbal communication skills include greeting others, gaining attention, asking for help, sharing, turn-taking, conversational skills, group work, problem-solving and making friends. Children who have social skills difficulties may struggle with many of these skills. For example, Melinda will actively set out to start arguments by targeting the area where children are playing by knocking over or destroying their block building, train tracks or playdough constructions. She will then wait for the child to say something and then start arguing with them that she didn't do it.

Intervention is critical for addressing the child's social skills.

Learning skills

Learning disability, learning disorder or specific learning disorder is a neurodevelopmental disorder that begins during school-age, affects the acquisition, organisation, retention, understanding or use of specific skills (e.g., reading, writing, and maths), which are the foundation for academic learning. Types of learning disorders include dyslexia (difficulty with reading), dysgraphia (difficulty with writing) and dyscalculia (difficulty with maths) (APA, 2013).

Learning disabilities result from impairments in one or more cognitive processes related to perceiving, thinking, remembering or learning. These include, but are not limited to, difficulties with language processing, phonological processing, visual spatial processing, processing speed, memory, attention and executive functions (e.g. planning, organising, sequencing and decision making)(British Columbia School Superintendents' Association, 2011). Children with learning difficulties experience repeated failure, rejection and frustration. For example, Justin has ADHD, dyslexia, dysgraphia and dyscalculia. He struggles with completing his classwork independently so will often argue with his teacher that he can't do the work as it is too babyish, boring and too easy. On the outside it looks argumentative but in reality, Justin is using his behaviour to save face and create a way to escape or avoid doing the work. Intervention is critical for addressing the child's learning skills.

Problem-solving skills

Problem-solving is a higher order thinking skill which requires critical and creative thinking.

To successfully problem-solve, a child first needs to identify the problem. This requires the child to differentiate between what is not a problem, a little problem, a medium problem or a big problem. Children who are argumentative use a one-size-fits-all approach which means they quickly jump to conclusions and thus can become argumentative about the things that would be considered by most as insignificant. For example, Bree sees malicious intent in the motives of her peer and withholds friendship if they don't give her their undivided attention, i.e. the peer must play exclusively with Bree and not play with the other children in the group. Bree would begin an argument with her peer which would end in her elbowing and kicking her peer under the table to let her know of her displeasure that she socialised with other children.

The next step in problem-solving involves generating solutions, controlling impulses, evaluating the consequences of the various solutions and identifying the best solution. The child may have difficulties with one or more of these steps which means they may act without thinking it through. For example, in art class Jonas was paired with another child to complete a painting. The other child ended up using all the green paint. Jonas started to argue with the other child. The teacher had to intervene and when she told Jonas he could mix blue and yellow paint to get green or come up to her and ask her or another group for green paint Jonas calmed down. Intervention is critical for addressing the child's problem-solving skills.

Interests, likes and dislikes

Knowing the child's interests, likes and dislikes can give insight into what may be triggering their argumentative behaviour. For example, Andrew is more likely to be focused, compliant and less argumentative when he knows that after he has completed a task he will be offered free time where he can choose what he wants to do.

Major life events the child has experienced

Have a discussion with the child's parents and caregivers, to discover if there have been changes in the child's family or home situation recently that might affect the child's behaviour (e.g. moving homes, new sibling being born or sibling moving out). In these situations, some children exhibit emotional and behavioural difficulties, but gradually return to their previous functioning over time. However, there are some events that can have severe and long-lasting events, namely traumatic events.

The Diagnostic and Statistical Manual of Mental Disorders 5th edition (DSM-5) [American Psychiatric Publishing (APA), 2013], is a handbook that is used by mental health professionals. The DSM-5 defines trauma as "Exposure to actual or threatened death, serious injury, or sexual violence in one (or more) of the following ways: directly experiencing the traumatic event(s); witnessing, in person, the traumatic event(s) as it occurred to others; learning that the traumatic event(s) occurred to a close family member or close friend (in case of actual or threatened death of a family member or friend, the event(s) must have been violent or accidental); or experiencing repeated or extreme exposure to aversive details of the traumatic event(s)" (APA, 2013, p. 271).

Children vary in their reactions and responses to traumatic events. It is important that children who have experienced one or more traumatic events (e.g. divorce, loss of a loved one and being bullied) receive ongoing support to work through their experiences. Without ongoing support, the stress related to the traumatic event lingers and alters the brain which can have lasting effects on the child's development, growth and functioning. This results in the child having difficulty with learning new skills and regressing by losing previously acquired skills causing changes in the child's cognitive, physical, social, emotional, communication and behavioural skills. Intervention is critical for helping the child develop these skills.

Describe the argumentative behaviour

Describe the argumentative behaviour in objective, specific and clear terms so that anyone who is not present has a clear picture of it. For example, instead of: 'Larry loves arguing', a better description would be: 'When asked to do something Larry will straightaway ask 'Why?' and then argue in a back and forth manner until the other person walks away.' The latter description is specific, observable and measurable so that anyone who is not present has a clear picture of it.

Before using direct methods of collecting data, it is important to ask people who know the child well about their view of when and where argumentative behaviour happens, who is involved when this behaviour occurs, when it is likely or unlikely to occur and why they think the child uses argumentative behaviour.

Use the *Child's Profile* form provided below to answer the questions as applicable. When answering the questions below describe as much detail as possible.

Child's Profile

Name	Date of birth
Contributor name	Contributor role
Address	Date completed

General health

Visual skills

Hearing skills

Physical skills

Sensory needs

Sleep patterns

Eating and drinking skills

Communication skills

Emotional regulation skills

Social skills

Learning skills

Problem-solving skills

Interests, likes and dislikes

Major life events the child has experienced

Describe the child's argumentative behaviour

Other comments

After completing the *child's profile*, the next type of assessment includes observing the child during real time and measuring the argumentative behaviour. This means noting the frequency, duration and intensity of the argumentative behaviour. Be sure to track this data over the course of at least a few weeks or longer.

Behaviour Data Collection Forms

By observing how the child interacts with various people, in different activities and in different environments, measurable dimensions of the argumentative behaviour can be gathered. Use the *Frequency* (how often it occurs), *Duration* (how long it can last) and *Intensity* (how severe it is) recording forms provided on the following pages to collate the data.

Behaviour Data Collection Form

Child name _____

Recorder name/s _____

Context: _____

Describe the behaviour: _____

Procedure: Document details of the argumentative behaviour as accurately as possible i.e. estimated start – finish time of argumentative behaviour, what the child's argumentative behaviour is about, where it happens and with whom it happens.

Date and estimated start – finish time of argumentative behaviour	Details of Incident
	What? Who? Where?
	What? Who? Where?
	What? Who? Where?
	What? Who? Where?
	What? Who? Where?
	What? Who? Where?

Based on the information collected, identify any patterns:

- When is the argumentative behaviour likely to occur?
- With whom is the child likely to become argumentative?
- Where is the child likely to exhibit argumentative behaviour?
- What tasks cause the child to exhibit argumentative behaviour?
- Are there any times of the day when the argumentative behaviour is:
  - Mild/low
  - Moderate/medium
  - Severe/high

Functional Behaviour Analysis (FBA)

A Functional Behaviour Analysis (FBA) is a systematic and collaborative problem-solving process (Ohio Department of Education, 2002). FBA involves reflecting on an incident when the argumentative behaviour occurred to identify what triggered it and the purpose (function) that the behaviour served). It is a process that aims to analyse the antecedents (what preceded the behaviour), the behaviour itself and the consequence (what happened immediately after the behaviour).

FBA → Complete 'Document incident'

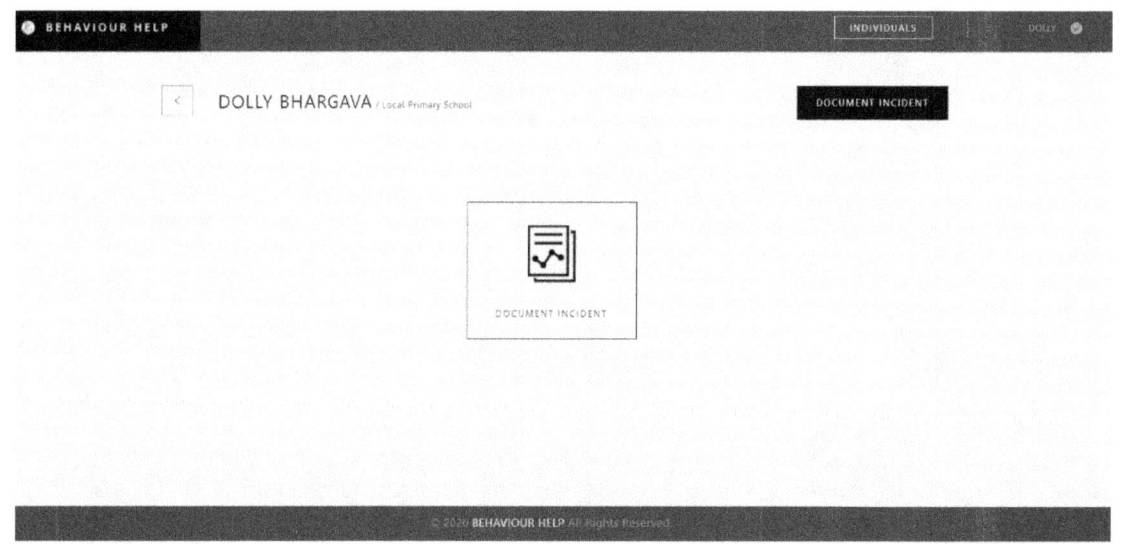

To complete the FBA, log on to the Behaviour Help web-based app (www.behaviourhelp.com/app/#/signup). The user can systematically analyse a recent incident by completing an FBA in the assessment section of the web-based app. Start by selecting 'document incident'. Alternatively, details can be recorded on paper using the *Antecedent – Behaviour – Consequence* form provided at the end of this section.

The following information shows what to include and how to answer the questions posed by the FBA.

FBA – Complete 'Record incident'

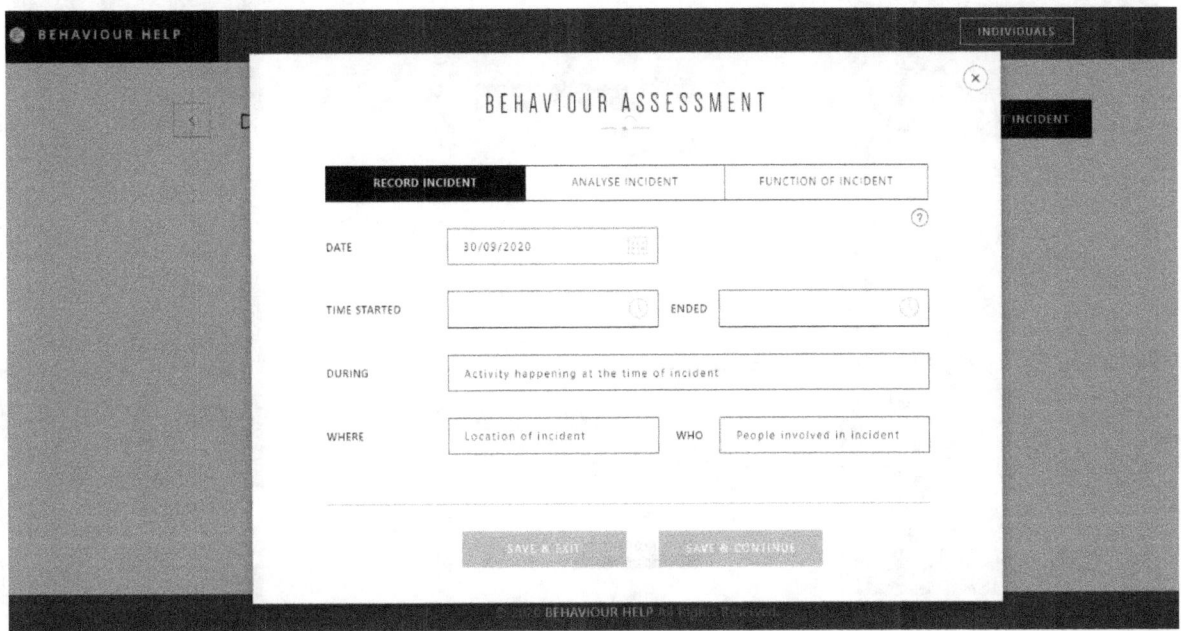

What?	Record the details of the incident.
Why?	These details will provide insight into the situation where the argumentative behaviour occurs.
How?	Record the information in the web-based app or in the *Antecedent – Behaviour – Consequence* form provided at the end of this section. Date – Record the date the incident occurred. Time started – Record the time the incident started. Ended – Record the time the incident finished. During – Record the activity that was happening at the time of the incident. Where – Record the location of the incident. Who- Record the names of people (children and adults) who were involved in the incident.

FBA —Complete 'Analyse incident'—Antecedent

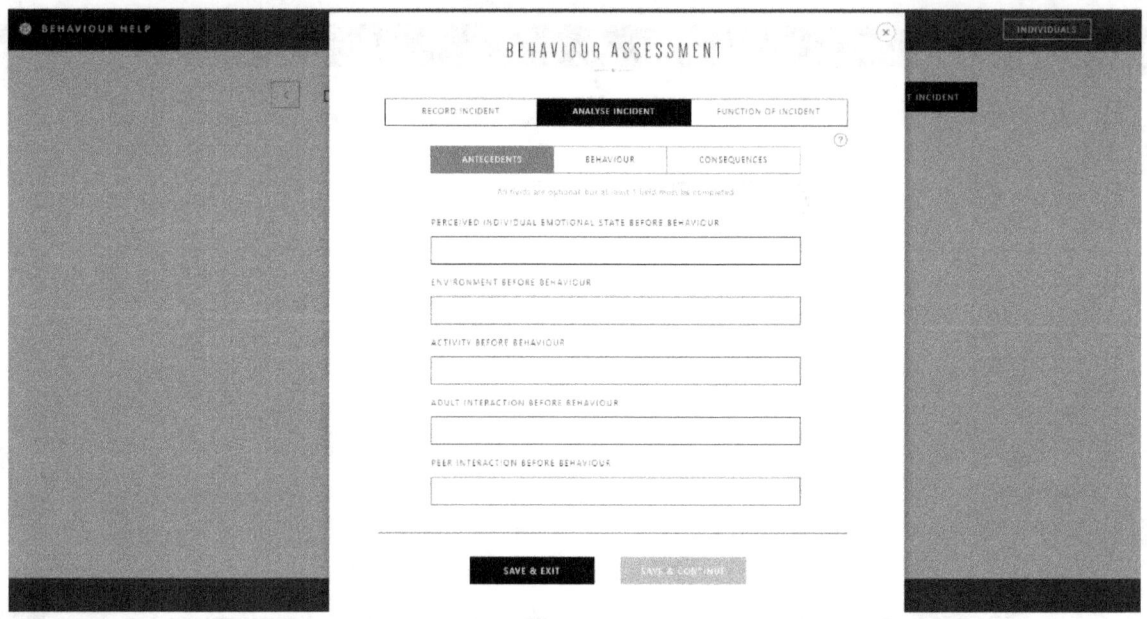

What?	Record the events (antecedents) that immediately preceded the argumentative behaviour.
Why?	It is important to identify what may have triggered the child's behaviour. This information can then be used to identify intervention strategies to prevent and manage the argumentative behaviour in the future.
How?	The next couple of pages provide a comprehensive list of potential triggers related to the child, interaction, activity or environment that could have contributed to the child's argumentative behaviour. With the help of the team, select the options that apply and/or edit the text as appropriate. Record the information in the *Antecedent – Behaviour – Consequence* form provided at the end of this section. . Alternatively, select from predefined triggers in the Behaviour Help web-based app and add any of the argumentative behaviour-customised triggers shown below.

Antecedent

Perceived child emotional state before argumentative behaviour	☐ Calm ☐ Happy ☐ Lonely ☐ Jealous

	☐ Unsafe ☐ Bored ☐ Stressed ☐ Overexcited ☐ Overstimulated ☐ Frustrated ☐ Tired ☐ Unwell ☐ Hungry ☐ Worried ☐ Scared ☐ Upset ☐ Angry ☐ Thirsty ☐ Tense ☐ In pain ☐ Uncomfortable ☐ Other
Environmental context before argumentative behaviour	<u>General aspects</u> ☐ Transition between environments ☐ Unfamiliar environment ☐ Non-preferred environment <u>Sensory aspects</u> *Tactile (touch) aspects* ☐ Too hot ☐ Too cold *Olfactory (smell) aspects* ☐ Strong odour ☐ Non-preferred odour ☐ Preferred odour *Proprioceptive (body awareness) aspects* ☐ Had insufficient personal space ☐ Too crowded *Auditory aspects* ☐ Too noisy

	☐ Too quiet *Visual aspects* ☐ Bright lights ☐ Too dark ☐ Visually cluttered ☐ Visually under stimulating ☐ Other
Peer context before argumentative behaviour	☐ Reacted to child ☐ Bullied child ☐ Touched child ☐ Touched child's belongings ☐ Reacted to child ☐ Left room ☐ Entered room ☐ Moved away ☐ Denied child request ☐ Ignored child ☐ Gave low levels of attention ☐ Gave high levels of attention ☐ Other
Adult context before argumentative behaviour	*Adult present* ☐ Preferred adult present ☐ Preferred adult absent ☐ Unfamiliar adult present ☐ Regular adult absent ☐ Non-preferred adult present *Adult attention* ☐ Moved away ☐ Moved closer ☐ Gave others attention ☐ Touched child ☐ Ignored child ☐ Gave low levels of attention ☐ Gave high levels of attention

	Adult communication ☐ Asked a question suddenly ☐ Gave inconsistent directions ☐ Gave unclear directions ☐ Gave complex directions ☐ Denied child request ☐ Offered assistance without asking ☐ Offered praise ☐ Used sarcasm ☐ Used negative tone of voice ☐ Raised voice ☐ Asked child to wait ☐ Backed child into a corner ☐ Insisted on having the last word ☐ Brought up unrelated events ☐ Made unsubstantiated accusations ☐ Attacked character ☐ Used unwarranted physical force ☐ Mimicked child ☐ Used tense body language ☐ Said 'no', 'not to', 'stop', 'don't' or 'wait' ☐ Used degrading, insulting, humiliating or embarrassing put downs ☐ Gave child corrective feedback ☐ Gave child negative feedback ☐ Other
Activity-context before argumentative behaviour	<u>General aspects</u> ☐ Requested activity denied ☐ Preferred activity stopped ☐ Disliked activity that was offered ☐ Activity started late ☐ Finished early ☐ Flow was interrupted ☐ Lost a game ☐ Failed in the activity ☐ Unexpected changes ☐ Unstructured ☐ Unfamiliar

- [ ] Difficult
- [ ] Easy
- [ ] Long
- [ ] Repetitive
- [ ] Group work
- [ ] Transitions
- [ ] Long waiting periods
- [ ] Insufficient equipment
- [ ] Incorrect equipment
- [ ] No decision-making opportunities
- [ ] Many decision-making opportunities
- [ ] Independent work
- [ ] Information about upcoming activity was not given
- [ ] Transition occurred without sufficient warning
- [ ] Transition was rushed
- [ ] Other

<u>Sensory aspects</u>

Visual aspects
- [ ] Preferred visual tasks
- [ ] Small font and size
- [x] Too much visual information
- [ ] Non-preferred visual tasks

Tactile (touch) aspects
- [ ] Too much touch
- [ ] Insufficient touch
- [ ] Unexpected touch
- [ ] Clothing seemed uncomfortable
- [ ] Disliked the textures of the activity materials
- [ ] Liked the textures of the activity materials
- [ ] Item involved preferred touch

Auditory (sound) aspects
- [ ] Equipment was too loud
- [ ] Too much auditory information
- [ ] Interrupted by sudden loud noises
- [ ] Non-preferred auditory elements

☐ Preferred auditory elements

Proprioceptive (body awareness) aspects
☐ Required postural control
☐ Did not provide sufficient heavy work/resistive input
☐ Complex motor planning/control and body awareness tasks
☐ Child's body position seemed uncomfortable
☐ Child's seating equipment seemed uncomfortable

Olfactory (smell) aspects
☐ Strong odour
☐ Non-preferred odour
☐ Preferred odour

Gustatory (taste) aspects
☐ Non-preferred taste
☐ Preferred taste
☐ Engagement with food items
☐ Preferred non-food items

Vestibular (movement) aspects
☐ Non-preferred movement tasks
☐ Did not include movement tasks
☐ Preferred movement tasks
☐ Too many movement tasks
☐ Other

FBA – Complete 'Analyse incident' – Behaviour

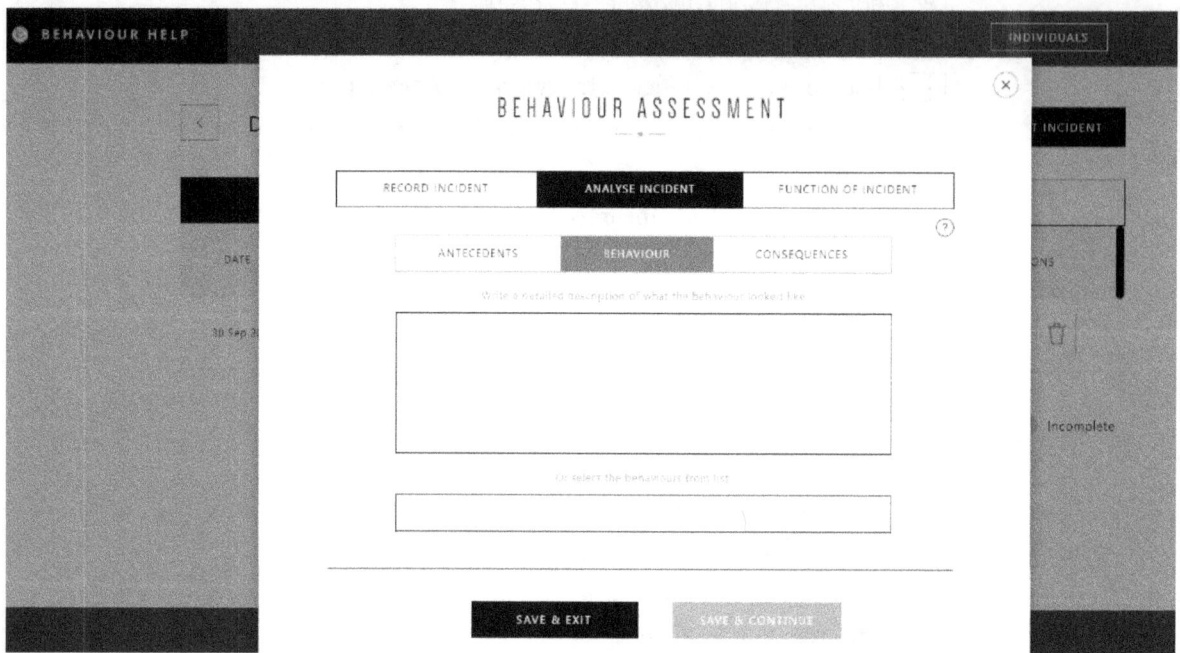

What?	Provide a description of the child's argumentative behaviour during the incident in observable and measurable terms.
Why?	Describing behaviour in these terms instead of a vague description will allow others who were not present to have a clear picture of what the argumentative behaviour looked like.
How?	With the help of the team, write a detailed description that is specific, observable and measurable. For example, 'At the end of the day when asked to pack away the materials, Larry straightaway asked 'Why?' and then argued in a back and forth manner until the other person walked away.' The description can be recorded in the web-based app or in the *Antecedent – Behaviour – Consequence* form provided at the end of this section. .

FBA —Complete 'Analyse incident' —Consequences

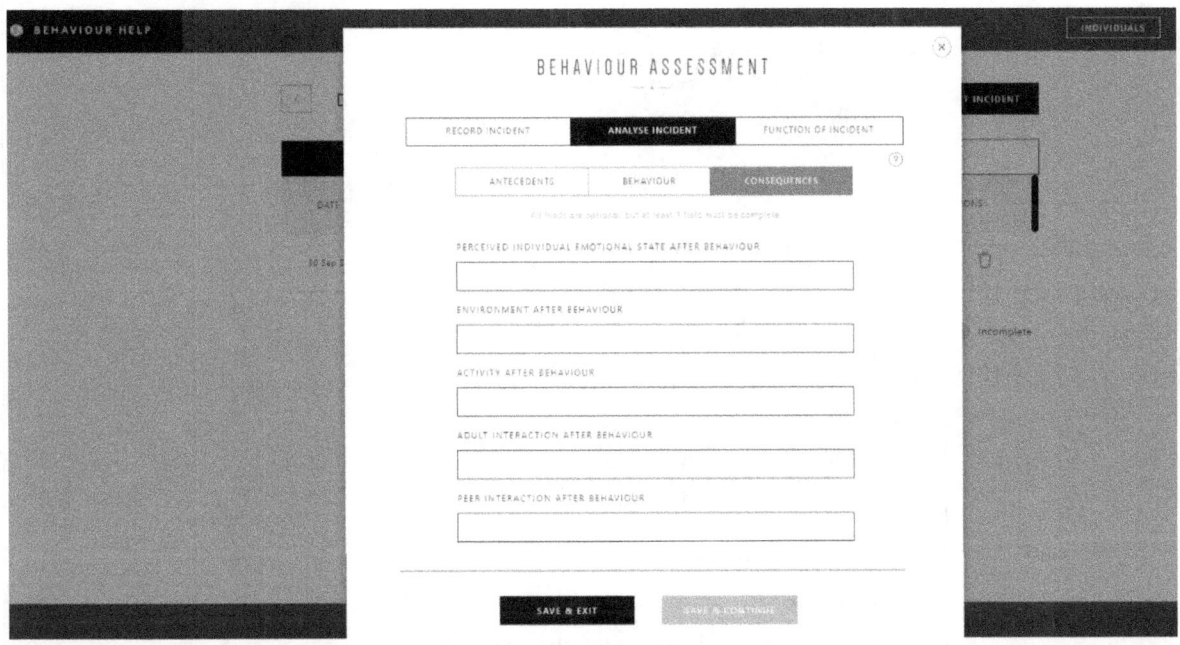

What?	Record the events (consequences) that followed the behaviour.
Why?	This will help identify the events following the argumentative behaviour that could be strengthening, maintaining or reinforcing it.
How?	As a team, identify which of the subheadings listed on the next few pages relate to the consequence/s of the child's behaviour. Record the information in the *Antecedent – Behaviour – Consequence* form provided at the end of this section. . Alternatively, select from predefined triggers in the Behaviour Help web-based app and add any of the argumentative behaviour-customised triggers shown below.

Consequences

Perceived child emotional state after argumentative behaviour	☐ Upset ☐ Worried ☐ Agitated ☐ Aroused ☐ Calm ☐ Better ☐ Satiated ☐ Thirst quenched

	☐ Comfortable
	☐ Rested
	☐ Safe
	☐ Relieved
	☐ Happy
	☐ Other
Environmental context after argumentative behaviour	<u>General aspects</u> ☐ Removed from environment ☐ Returned to preferred environment <u>Sensory aspects</u> *Tactile (touch) aspects* ☐ Temperature was increased ☐ Temperature was decreased *Olfactory (smell) aspects* ☐ Moved to an environment with decreased odour ☐ Moved to an environment with preferred odour *Auditory aspects* ☐ Moved to a quieter environment ☐ Moved to a noisier environment *Proprioceptive (body awareness) aspects* ☐ Offered personal space ☐ Moved away from others *Visual aspects* ☐ Moved to an environment with dimmer lights ☐ Moved to an environment with brighter lights ☐ Moved to an environment with less clutter ☐ Moved to an environment with more visual stimulation ☐ Other
Peer context after argumentative behaviour	☐ Ignored child ☐ Higher levels of attention ☐ Lower levels of attention ☐ Moved away from the child ☐ Reprimanded for bullying behaviour ☐ Other

Adult context after argumentative behaviour	☐ Other familiar adult entered room ☐ Low levels of attention ☐ High levels of attention ☐ Gave others attention ☐ Stopped what they were doing ☐ Ignored child ☐ Moved away ☐ Moved closer ☐ Touched child ☐ Preferred adult moved closer ☐ Left child alone ☐ Gave child access to preferred items ☐ Used sarcasm ☐ Used negative tone of voice ☐ Raised voice ☐ Used unwarranted physical force ☐ Talked ☐ Gave clearer directions ☐ Gave simpler directions ☐ Gave requested item ☐ Other
Activity context after argumentative behaviour	<u>General aspects</u> ☐ Easier activity was offered ☐ Correct equipment was offered ☐ Preferred activity continued ☐ Preferred activity was offered ☐ Child left alone to work by themselves ☐ Requested activity was provided ☐ Activity was ceased ☐ Removed from activity ☐ Offered choice of other activities ☐ Non-preferred activity was discontinued <u>Sensory aspects</u> *Olfactory (smell) aspects* ☐ Non-preferred odour removed ☐ Preferred odour offered

Visual aspe\cts
- ☐ Offered preferred visual tasks
- ☐ Offered an activity with reduced visual content

Auditory (sound) aspects
- ☐ Loud equipment was removed
- ☐ Moved away from loud equipment
- ☐ Offered preferred auditory items
- ☐ Auditory information in activity reduced
- ☐ Preferred auditory items offered
- ☐ Non-preferred auditory items removed

Gustatory (taste) aspects
- ☐ Non-preferred taste removed
- ☐ Preferred taste offered
- ☐ Preferred non-edible items consumed
- ☐ Food items removed

Vestibular (movement) aspects
- ☐ Movement tasks offered
- ☐ Movement tasks ceased
- ☐ Movement tasks reduced

Tactile (touch) aspects
- ☐ Deep pressure touch offered
- ☐ Light pressure touch offered
- ☐ Comfortable clothing offered
- ☐ Body position changed
- ☐ Uncomfortable clothing removed
- ☐ Items with preferred touch offered
- ☐ Different seating equipment offered
- ☐ Items with non-preferred touch removed
- ☐ Other

FBA – Complete 'Analyse incident' – Incident function

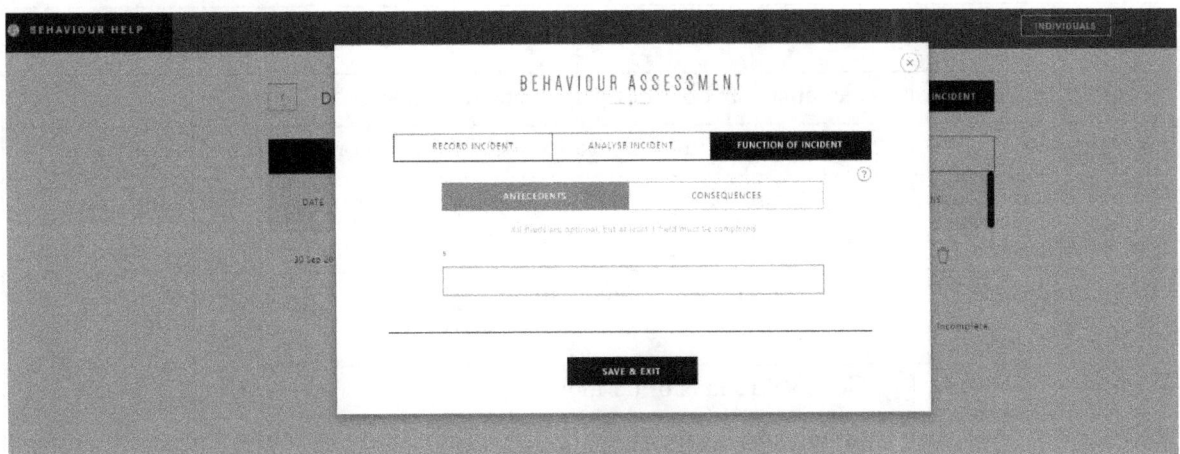

What?	Reflect on the antecedents (what preceded the behaviour) and consequences (what happened immediately after the behaviour) to determine the function/s (purpose) of the argumentative behaviour and create a hypothesis.
Why?	By understanding the purpose of the argumentative behaviour, the antecedents or the consequences can be addressed to prevent the occurrence of the behaviour. The child can also be taught the appropriate alternative behaviour they can use to achieve the purpose instead of the argumentative behaviour.
How?	It is important to remember that the one behaviour may serve different functions at different times. Identify which of the subheadings listed on the next page describe the function/s of the argumentative behaviour within the incident. If recorded on paper, complete the Antecedent-Behaviour-Consequence form provided at the end of this section. . Alternatively, select from predefined functions in the Behaviour Help web-based app and add any of the behaviour-customised functions shown below.

Incident functions

Function	The child engages in the argumentative behaviour to:
Tangible	☐ Get/obtain an object or participate in an activity
Attention	☐ Get/obtain positive or negative social attention or interaction from another.
Sensory input or stimulation	☐ Get/obtain some form of sensory input or stimulation (i.e. visual, auditory, olfactory, gustatory, tactile, vestibular or proprioceptive).
Power/influence/ control	☐ Get/obtain power to cause, direct or prevent actions/reactions/events.
Status	☐ Get/obtain a rank or position
Revenge	☐ Get/obtain revenge for the perceived or real hurt or harm caused by someone else.
Escape	☐ Avoid/get away from receiving an object or participating in an activity. ☐ Avoid/get away from positive or negative social attention or interaction from another. ☐ Avoid/get away from receiving some form of sensory input or stimulation. ☐ Avoid/get away from having the ability to make or prevent actions/reactions/events from happening. ☐ Avoid/get away from obtaining a rank or position.

Antecedent-Behaviour-Consequence Form

Child name _____ Date _____

Recorder name/s _____

During (Activity happening at the time of incident) _____

Time started _____ Time ended _____

Where (Location of incident) _____

Who (people involved in incident) _____

	Antecedent	Behaviour	Consequence	Hypothesised Function
Perceived individual state				
Environment				
Activity				
Adult interaction				
Peer interaction				

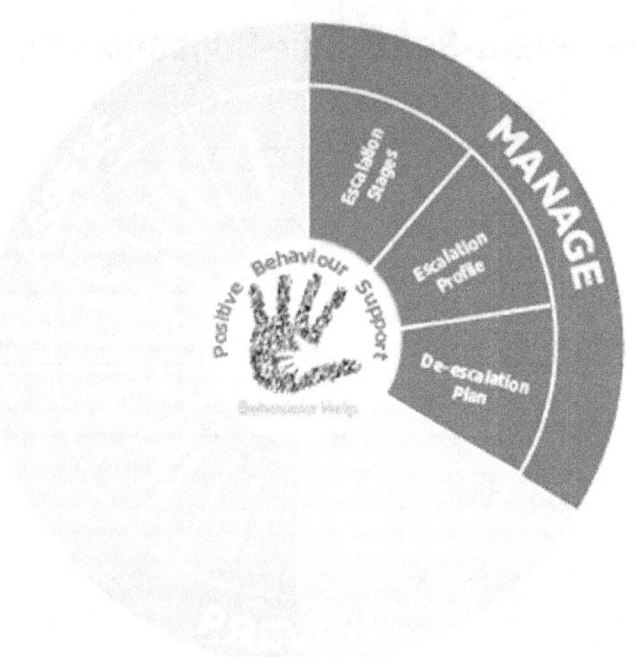

6. MANAGE STAGE

When a child exhibits argumentative behaviour, some children escalate if they are not responded to in a planned manner. Hence, it is important to create a comprehensive management plan that outlines how to effectively respond to the argumentative behaviour. This can help to safely defuse, redirect and de-escalate the situation in the least disruptive manner.

The Manage stage involves the team working through the checklist tasks listed:

Manage Stage Checklist:

- Escalation stages – Help those supporting the child to recognise the number of stages the child exhibits as their emotion rises (i.e. mild escalation, moderate escalation, extreme escalation and recovery stage).
- Escalation profile– Help those supporting the child to recognise what non-verbal and/or verbal behaviours are exhibited in the different escalation stages and how long it can last.

- De-escalation plan – Help those supporting the child with guidelines on how to immediately respond when the behaviour occurs, safely defuse and de-escalate the situation in the least disruptive manner.

To get started, go to the Behaviour Help web-based app, click on the intervention tab and then click on a new behaviour profile or, if paper is preferred, use the forms provided on the following pages.

Escalation Stages

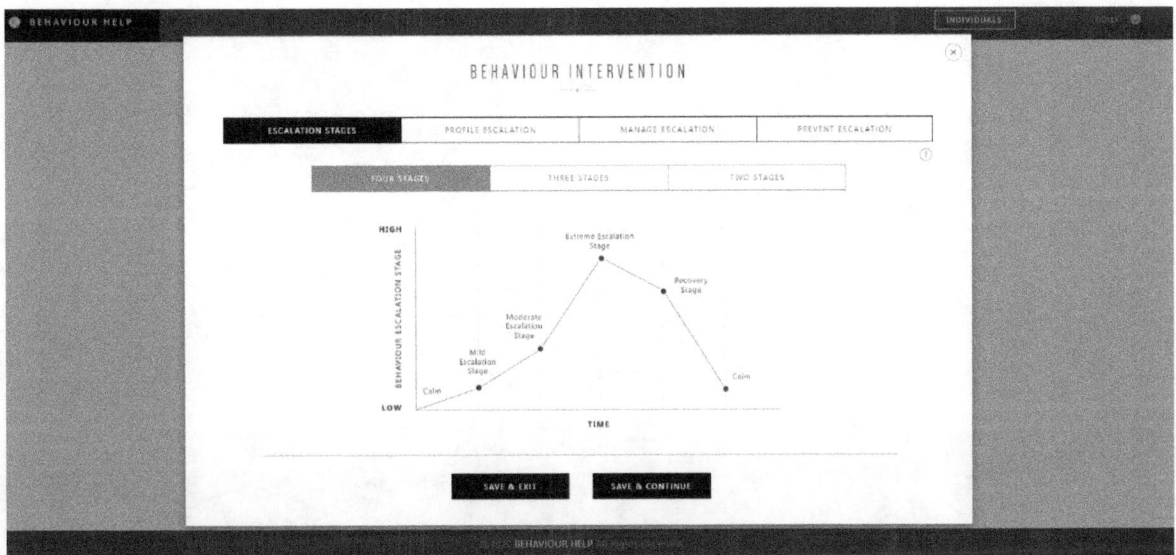

As a child's level of emotion intensity (strength) increases, the behaviour escalates.

This escalation can be seen in stages:

- Calm stage - the child is relatively calm, composed and cooperative.
- Mild escalation stage - the child becomes increasingly unfocused, upset and stressed.
- Moderate escalation stage - the child is non-compliant, confrontational and less logical.
- Extreme escalation stage - the child is out of control, irrational and needs to rage it out.
- Recovery stage - the child calms down and is willing to participate in activities.

Each child is unique and experiences the escalation stages differently. The child may go through all four stages or only some stages. Chart the escalation stages for the child by identifying and selecting the number of stages the child experiences (e.g. five, four, three or two stages) in the Behaviour Help web-based app. Alternatively, the observed stages can be marked on the *Escalation Stages* form below.

Escalation Stages Form

Child name _____ Date _____

Recorder name/s _____

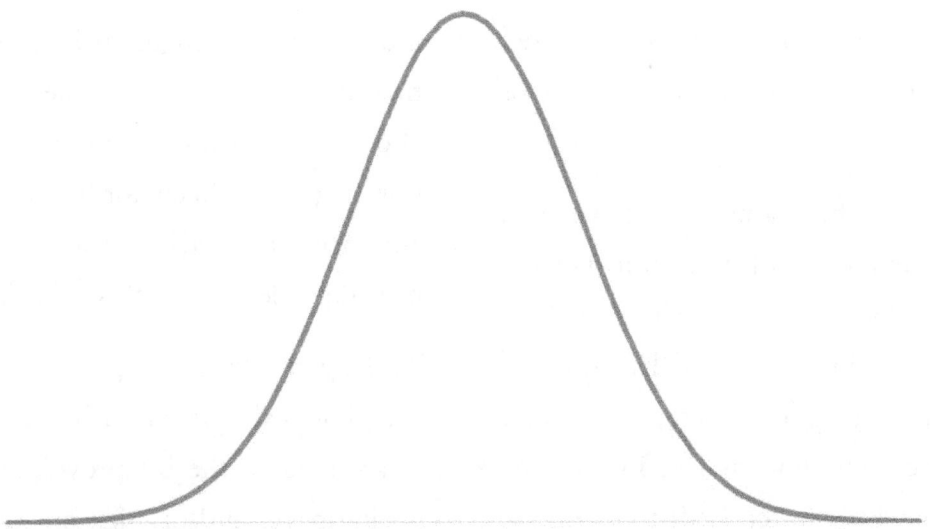

Escalation Profile

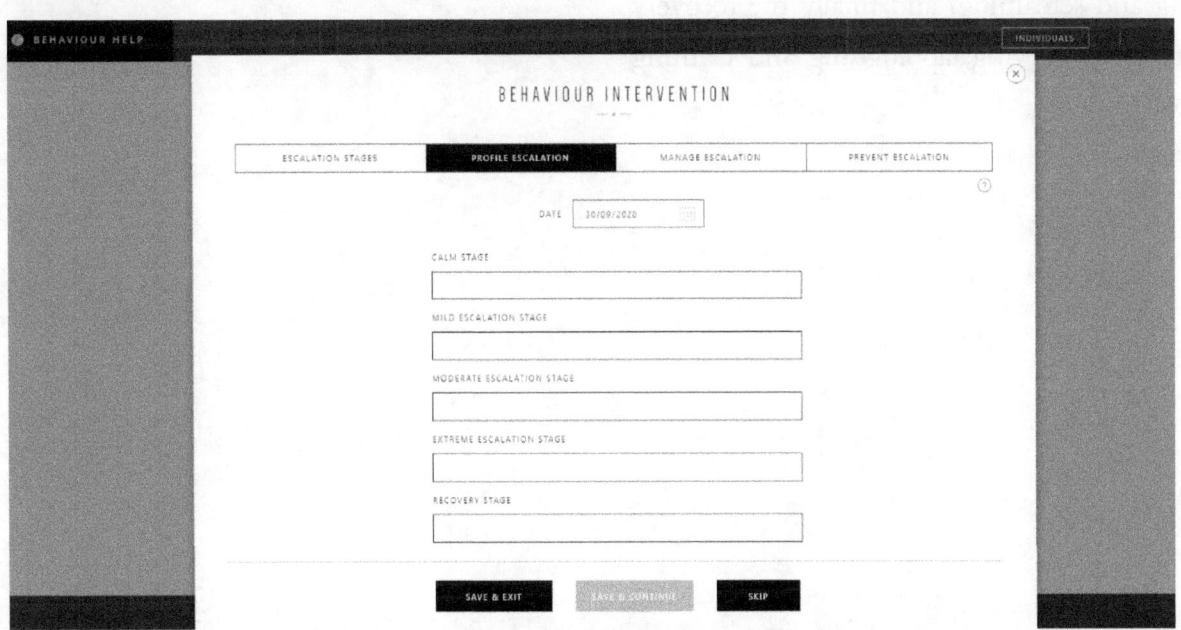

Once the number of escalation stages the child experiences has been charted, the next step is to identify the non-verbal and/or verbal behaviours the child exhibits in each stage. The child may exhibit behaviours that are directed towards the external environment and/or behaviours that are directed towards the self in the different stages of escalation.

The child will exhibit a range of behaviours in the different stages of escalation. For example, a child will go from a calm stage (e.g. quiet voice, staying seated and listening) to mild escalation (e.g. loud voice, throwing a book on the floor and standing in a defensive posture with arms crossed) to moderate escalation (e.g. swearing, arguing and pacing) to extreme escalation (e.g. hitting, kicking and screaming) and finally the recovery stage (e.g. crying, apologising and calming down).

Develop an escalation profile plan with the team, by identifying and selecting externalised and internalised behaviours the child exhibits in each stage. Externalised challenging behaviours are those that are directed towards the external environment and/or internalised challenging behaviours are those that are directed towards the self. This will also help the team recognise at what escalation stage/s it is likely for the child to exhibit argumentative behaviour and recognise the behaviours leading to this behaviour.

To help the team recognise the behaviours the child exhibits in each escalation stage please refer to the list provided on the following pages and/or click on 'Or select the behaviours from the escalation stage list' in the web-based app.

Externalised challenging behaviours

Aggressive behaviour	<u>Verbally aggressive behaviours</u> ☐ Attempting to draw people into a power struggle ☐ Attempting to draw people into an argument ☐ Interrupting others ☐ Provoking a confrontation ☐ Screaming at others ☐ Swearing at others ☐ Threatening others ☐ Yelling out inappropriate comments <u>Physically aggressive behaviours</u> ☐ Biting ☐ Choking ☐ Hitting ☐ Kicking ☐ Pinching ☐ Pulling hair ☐ Punching ☐ Pushing ☐ Scratching ☐ Stealing ☐ Tripping ☐ Other
Disorganised behaviour	☐ Compulsive ☐ Dropping to the floor ☐ Frantic ☐ Overactive ☐ Pausing between actions ☐ Restless ☐ Running away ☐ Other
Disruptive behaviour	☐ Bragging ☐ Chronic blurting out ☐ Clowning around

	☐ Copying another's speech
	☐ Frequently making noises
	☐ Hand raising all the time
	☐ Inappropriate sexual behaviour
	☐ Laughing inappropriately
	☐ Lying
	☐ Making prejudicial remarks: ○ Religious ○ Sexual orientation ○ Racial
	☐ Needing someone to help, teach or watch them do something
	☐ Repeatedly seeking validation
	☐ Spreading rumours
	☐ Talking excessively
	☐ Tattling
	☐ Teasing
	☐ Telling fantastical stories
	☐ Using a loud and animated voice
	☐ Other
Self-injurious behaviour	☐ Banging
	☐ Biting
	☐ Burning
	☐ Cutting
	☐ Ingesting dangerous substance
	☐ Inhaling dangerous substance
	☐ Overdosing on medication
	☐ Picking
	☐ Poking
	☐ Refusing food
	☐ Refusing medication
	☐ Scratching
	☐ Slapping
	☐ Twisting
	☐ Other
Destructive behaviour	☐ Breaking
	☐ Burning
	☐ Damaging
	☐ Graffitiing

	☐ Overturning ☐ Picking ☐ Pulling apart ☐ Smashing ☐ Stealing ☐ Tearing ☐ Throwing ☐ Other
Self-stimulatory behaviour	<u>Proprioceptive</u> ☐ Biting self ☐ Chewing on things ☐ Crashing into people ☐ Crashing into things ☐ Grinding teeth ☐ Slamming things <u>Gustatory</u> ☐ Eating non-food items ☐ Licking objects ☐ Mouthing objects ☐ Placing body part in mouth ☐ Placing object in mouth ☐ Regurgitating ☐ Ruminating <u>Olfactory</u> ☐ Holding nose ☐ Smelling objects ☐ Sniffing people <u>Vestibular</u> ☐ Swinging ☐ Tapping foot ☐ Flapping hands ☐ Spinning ☐ Pacing ☐ Bouncing ☐ Rocking front to back

- [ ] Rocking side to side

<u>Auditory</u>
- [ ] Repetitive questioning
- [ ] Giggling inappropriately
- [ ] Grunting or high-pitched shrieking
- [ ] Repeating phrases, movies quotes, song lyrics, etc.
- [ ] Making loud and/or high-pitched noises
- [ ] Making vocal sounds
- [ ] Banging objects
- [ ] Snapping fingers
- [ ] Tapping ears or objects
- [ ] Humming
- [ ] Covering ears

<u>Visual</u>
- [ ] Flicking fingers
- [ ] Lining things up
- [ ] Looking sideways at things
- [ ] Flapping hands
- [ ] Staring at lights or objects
- [ ] Repetitively blinking
- [ ] Turning on and off light switches
- [ ] Shaking things
- [ ] Throwing or dropping objects
- [ ] Doing a task repetitively
- [ ] Wiggling fingers in front or at side of face
- [ ] Tilting head while watching objects
- [ ] Watching moving objects
- [ ] Waving fingers in front or at side of face
- [ ] Opening and shutting objects
- [ ] Stacking and knocking things down
- [ ] Pacing
- [ ] Spinning things
- [ ] Twirling objects
- [ ] Twirling self
- [ ] Spinning self
- [ ] Walking in patterns

- ☐ Excessive drawing
- ☐ Watching same video repeatedly

<u>Tactile</u>
- ☐ Banging head
- ☐ Biting fingernails
- ☐ Biting self
- ☐ Chewing fingernails
- ☐ Chewing on insides of cheeks
- ☐ Chewing skin
- ☐ Clapping hands
- ☐ Grabbing someone's arm with both hands
- ☐ Grinding teeth
- ☐ Masturbating
- ☐ Mouthing objects
- ☐ Picking skin
- ☐ Pinching self
- ☐ Rubbing clothing between fingers
- ☐ Rubbing face
- ☐ Rubbing hands
- ☐ Rubbing skin
- ☐ Rubbing skin with object
- ☐ Scratching skin
- ☐ Spitting
- ☐ Squeezing head against arm
- ☐ Tapping body part
- ☐ Tapping object
- ☐ Wringing hands
- ☐ Other

Internalised challenging behaviours

- [ ] Appearing excessively shy
- [ ] Appearing sad most of the time
- [ ] Avoiding tasks
- [ ] Avoiding interactions
- [ ] Being indecisive
- [ ] Being excessively timid
- [ ] Being non-responsive
- [ ] Being reluctant to participate
- [ ] Being tearful
- [ ] Engaging in socially isolating behaviours
- [ ] Frequent complaints of pain such as stomach aches, headaches, dizziness or chest pain or illness
- [ ] Hiding behind furniture
- [ ] Hiding under furniture
- [ ] Repeated pleas to call home or go home
- [ ] Seeming excessively embarrassed
- [ ] Seeming excessively fearful
- [ ] Seeming excessively worried
- [ ] Withdrawn
- [ ] Other

Alternatively, details can be recorded on paper using the *Escalation Profile* form provided on the next page.

Escalation Profile Form

Child name _____ Date _____

Recorder name/s _____

Calm Stage

Mild Escalation Stage

Moderate Escalation Stage

Extreme Escalation Stage

Recovery Stage

De-escalation Plan

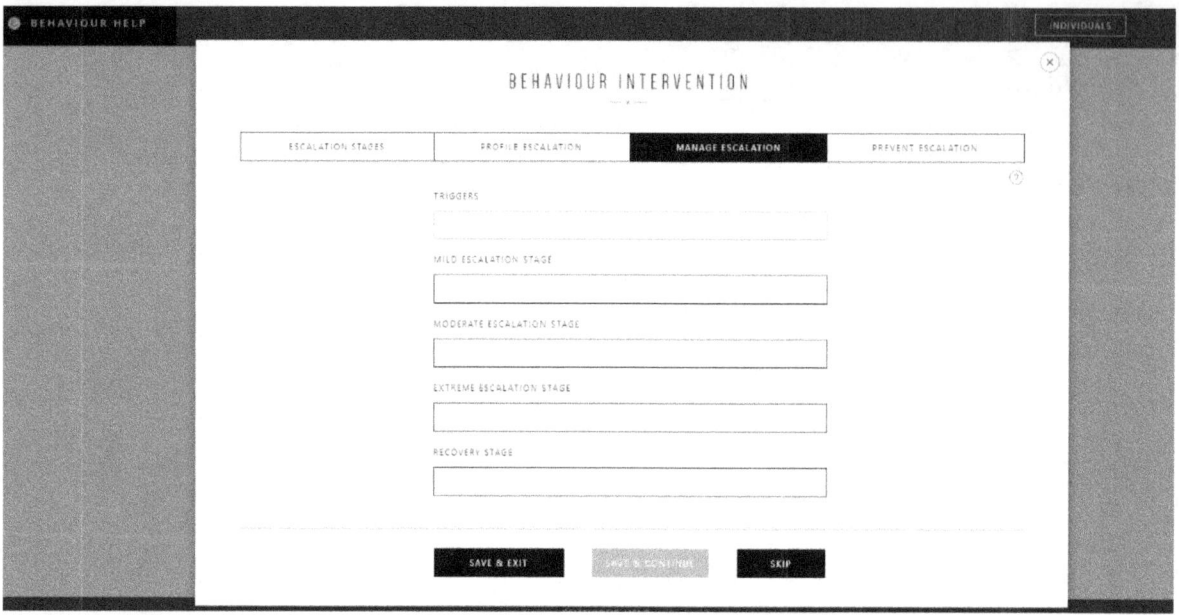

Develop a plan that the team can use to immediately respond to when the child exhibits argumentative behaviour.

The strategies to manage the argumentative behaviour are summarised by the acronym **DE-ESCALATION**:

Display calm demeanour
Engage attention
Encourage cooperation
Space to calm
Comfort, support and reassure
Ask what happened
Listen actively and attentively
Acknowledge and validate
Talk about positive attitudes, choices and behaviours
Identify appropriate alternate behaviour
Offer help
Note positives

The explanations for the DE-ESCALATION strategies are provided. Discuss them with the team, select and edit the strategies as appropriate. Not all strategies will suit or meet the child's needs, so select and tailor them based on the advice from the team. If recorded on paper, complete the *De-escalation plan* form provided at the end of this section. . In the app, the headings 'Triggers', 'Mild escalation stage', 'Moderate escalation stage', 'Extreme escalation stage' and 'Recovery stage' are used.

With the team, firstly record the triggers for the behaviour. Secondly, depending on the number of escalation stages the child exhibits and the range of other challenging behaviours the child exhibits in conjunction with argumentative behaviour, work as a team to identify stage-specific de-escalation strategies. This will enable everyone to take charge of the situation by safely bringing it under control and avoid further escalation of the child's behaviour in consistent ways.

DE-ESCALATION plan → **Display calm demeanour**

What?	Project calm, relaxed and positive body language as you discreetly observe the child.
Why?	Staying calm allows one to think clearly and make better decisions and responses. A calm composure also helps to transfer a sense of calm onto the child.
How?	☐ Take deep breaths. ☐ Appear calm. ☐ Maintain a relaxed facial expression. ☐ Maintain a safe distance from the child. ☐ Stand up straight with head up, feet about shoulder width apart and weight evenly balanced (if standing). ☐ Minimise sudden body movements. ☐ Place your hands in front of your body in an open and relaxed position. ☐ Do not turn your back to the child. ☐ Do not pace, fidget or shift your weight. ☐ Do not cross arms, place hands on hips, hands in pockets or arms behind back. ☐ Do not point or shake your finger at the child. ☐ Do not use aggressive facial expressions or smile.

DE-ESCALATION plan → **Engage attention, Encourage cooperation**

What?	Strategically select which arguments to respond to and get involved in.
Why?	By being intentional in terms of selectively responding and getting involved in the child's argumentative behaviour we can avoid escalating the situation. Also, by not responding to every argument we can avoid reinforcing the behaviour/s by giving it attention (positive or negative). By being selective of arguments to ignore or respond to, we can also reduce the overall amount of time being spent arguing which can negatively impact on the relationship with the child, and how the child views others. Instead, allow for more positive interactions that can help restore the relationship.
How?	<u>Categorise the child's topics of arguments into green, orange and red topics based on their importance:</u> ☐ Green – are topics that in the big scheme of things are not worth battling over. For example, if a child argues that the colour of the sky is pink, or they want to read a book back to front, or they do not want to use an eraser and instead just want to cross off the error. When a child brings up the argument the aim is to resolve it immediately by not entering the argument. ☐ Orange - are topics that in the big scheme of things are worth battling over. For example, the child is expected to come to the mat, the child has been asked to pack away their materials or the child is asked to move away from a peer. When a child begins to argue, the aim is to try and resolve it, but if after a while it doesn't appear to get resolved and the child begins to escalate then the aim for that moment is to safely defuse, redirect and de-escalate the situation. The aim is to create a win-win situation. The win for the child is that they get to solve the argument based on their preference but the win for everyone else is that a meltdown has not been induced or endured. However, at a later time when the child is calm it is important to spend 1:1 to reflect on the situation and avoid its reoccurrence. ☐ Red - are topics that in the big scheme of things are worth battling over and need to be immediately addressed for everyone's safety. For example, if a child is making threats and becoming physically aggressive, the argumentative behaviour needs to be addressed immediately for everyone's safety. Stay calm and rationally decide on the value of the topic being argued before responding. <u>Green strategies:</u> ☐ Do not stand in front facing the child. ☐ Standing side by side or sitting side by side is less confrontational.

- [ ] Avoid making sustained eye contact (i.e. longer than 2-3 seconds).
- [ ] Make eye contact from time to time.
- [ ] Lower the volume and pitch of your voice.
- [ ] Talk calmly, clearly, and slowly to tell your child what you want them to do, not what you don't want them to do. For example, say, 'Please talk to me using an inside voice' instead of 'Stop yelling!'
- [ ] Remain patient as the child puts forward their argument.
- [ ] Do not criticise, threaten, blame or put down the child.
- [ ] Listen actively and openly without judging, half listening or making assumptions about what the child is feeling or thinking.
- [ ] Acknowledge and empathise with the child's complaints, objections and criticisms.
- [ ] Reflect their argument back to them to make sure you have understood their perspective.
- [ ] Do not respond to the child's questions by adding any further explanations or offering any more choices or discussions.
- [ ] Explain that the solution they have chosen will suffice or 'agree to disagree'.
- [ ] Inform the child that the discussion is now paused and if they wish to have a discussion later on, they can schedule time with you.
- [ ] Inform the child of the activity that needs to be re-engaged in.

<u>Orange strategies:</u>
- [ ] Do not stand in front facing the child.
- [ ] Standing side by side or sitting side by side is less confrontational.
- [ ] Avoid making sustained eye contact (i.e. longer than 2-3 seconds).
- [ ] Make eye contact from time to time.
- [ ] Lower the volume and pitch of your voice.
- [ ] Use short sentences and pause between them.
- [ ] Talk calmly, clearly and slowly to tell the child what you want them to do, not what you don't want them to do. For example, say 'Please talk to me using an inside voice.' instead of 'Stop yelling!'.
- [ ] Remain patient as the child puts forward their argument.
- [ ] Do not criticise, threaten, blame or put down the child.
- [ ] Listen actively and openly without judging, half listening or making assumptions about what the child is feeling or thinking.
- [ ] Acknowledge and empathise with the child's complaints, objections and criticisms.

	☐ Reflect their argument back to them to make sure you have understood their perspective.
	☐ Use clarifying questions to better understand their perspective. For example, 'Can you tell me more about why ….'
	☐ Try to work towards a resolution by briefly explaining to the child your position of why you can or can't do something. For example, 'The school rules state… I wish I could change the rule but I don't make the rules.' Or 'I understand where you are coming from. In my position I can offer you two choices… or …'
	☐ Try to work towards a resolution.
	☐ Give the child time to process the information.
	☐ Avoid the back and forth of the argument trap.
	☐ Brief explanations should be repeated if the arguing continues.
	☐ Once the main points of the argument have been made, do not add more points or explanations, as this will open up more lines of attack for the child.
	☐ Ignore the child's behaviour as long as there are no safety concerns.
	☐ Inform the child that the discussion is now paused and if they wish to have a discussion later on they can make time with you.
	☐ Inform the child of the activity that needs to be re-engaged in.
	☐ Change adult interacting with child, if possible.
	☐ If the behaviour continues progress to 'Space to calm' strategy.
	<u>Red strategies:</u>
	☐ Encourage peers to minimise interaction with the child.
	☐ Encourage other adult/s to minimise interaction with the child.
	☐ Progress to 'Space to calm' strategy.

DE-ESCALATION plan → **Space to calm**

What?	Give the child space and time to calm down.
Why?	To ensure the safety and well-being of the child and everyone around the child it is important to give everyone space. By providing space it allows the child to recover, regain composure and regain control over their emotions and behaviour.
How?	☐ Make time immediately to support the child. ☐ Direct the child to the designated calm down, chill out, or sensory area. ☐ If it is difficult to support and/or supervise the child immediately, accompany the child to a supervised environment (e.g. school counsellor, school psychologist or administration office).

- [ ] Alternatively, provide the child with space by sending others away from the area.
- [ ] Remove potentially harmful objects.
- [ ] Maintain a reasonable distance from the child (left alone or needs adult present in space).
- [ ] Allow the child time to rage it out.
- [ ] Position yourself closer to the room entrance so you can make a quick exit if required.
- [ ] Minimise sudden body movements such as gestures, pacing and fidgeting.
- [ ] Place hands in front of the body in an open and relaxed position.
- [ ] Give no or minimal eye contact.
- [ ] Do not take the behaviours personally by remembering it's about the child's own upset and skills gap.
- [ ] Do not stand in front facing the child.
- [ ] Do not turn your back to the child.
- [ ] Do not pace, fidget or shift your weight.
- [ ] Do not touch the child.
- [ ] Do not allow the child to block your exit from the room.
- [ ] Do not cross arms, place hands on hips, hands in pockets or arms behind back.
- [ ] Do not point or shake your finger at the child.
- [ ] Do not use aggressive facial expressions or smile
- [ ] Engage in minimal or no talking.
- [ ] Ensure that if instructions have to be given, they are kept short and simple.
- [ ] State the instruction as a positive (do statement) rather than a negative (don't statement).
- [ ] Speak slowly in a calm, low and monotonous voice.
- [ ] Ignore and disregard the child's inappropriate language
- [ ] Do not raise your voice, yell or scream at the child.
- [ ] Do not argue, judge, interrupt or deny what the child says.
- [ ] Do not insult, criticise or shame the child.
- [ ] Do not discipline.
- [ ] Allow the child time to recover.
- [ ] Be aware that recovery can take up to 45 minutes or longer.

DE-ESCALATION plan → **Comfort, support and reassurance**

What?	Offer comfort, support and reassurance to the child.
Why?	The best way to support children during their times of distress is by allowing them to express their feelings. By being present the adult can gently guide the child to work through their emotions in healthy ways. Supporting the child in ways that is accepting of their experience and emotion will allow the child to trust, feel safe and strengthen the relationship. This will provide the platform for the child to pay attention to what the adult is saying and cooperate with their suggestions.
How?	☐ Stand side by side or sit side by side when talking to the child to be less confrontational. ☐ Avoid making sustained eye contact (more than 2-3 seconds at a time). ☐ Make eye contact from time to time. ☐ Lower the volume and pitch of voice. ☐ Keep tone even and firm. ☐ Speak at a slower pace. ☐ Respectfully and calmly let the child know you are there to listen, support and assist them in all situations (positive and negative). ☐ Connect by considering the underlying emotion behind the child's behaviour based on how they are currently experiencing things from their point of view. For example, 'I can see you are feeling _____'. ☐ Actively listen to the child. ☐ Paraphrase by repeating the message back to your child so that you can show that you listened and check that you understood. For example, 'You feel like nobody is understanding you', or 'You are feeling annoyed because _____'. ☐ Actively listen to the child. ☐ Explain to the child that it is important to calm down before talking and sorting through whatever is concerning them. ☐ Ask the child if they would like to do something that would make them feel better. ☐ Ask the child if they would like to use relaxation strategies (e.g. deep breathing, counting from 1 to 10, drink of water, mindfulness exercises or listening to soothing music) to calm down. ☐ Ask the child if they would like sensory activities to help them calm down. ☐ Ask the child if they would like to go for a walk. ☐ Use humour to lighten the mood.

DE-ESCALATION plan → **Ask what happened, Listen actively and attentively**

What?	Ask the child to explain what happened from their perspective.
Why?	To provide support that is sensitive and responsive to the child's needs it is important to tune into and view the situation from their perspective. Listening to the child attentively and fully is essential to relationship building.
How?	☐ Wait for the child to fully recover. ☐ Talk about the argumentative behaviour you have observed. ☐ Use a neutral and objective statement to enquire about the child's needs and concerns (e.g. 'Please tell me what is going on?', 'Can you tell me what is making you feel ___?' or 'Can you help me understand what happened?' or 'I wonder what caused you to ___'). ☐ Listen to both verbal and non-verbal communication with openness to understand what the child is going through. ☐ Paraphrase by repeating the message back to the child to check they have been understood. ☐ Do not insult, criticise or shame the child by making remarks that are patronising/belittling/dismissive (e.g. 'Don't worry' 'Calm down', 'Turn that frown upside down', 'You shouldn't feel that way', 'Nobody else feels like that' or 'It'll be okay). ☐ Clarify by asking open ended questions to get the complete picture of their concerns. ☐ Do not argue, judge, interrupt or deny what the child says. ☐ Do not raise voice, yell or scream at the child.

DE-ESCALATION plan → **Acknowledge and validate**

What?	Acknowledge and validate the child's emotions and thoughts.
Why?	Acknowledging and validating the child's emotions and thoughts makes them feel visible, heard and that they are important.
How?	☐ Use empathetic phrases that validate and acknowledge the child's feelings (e.g. 'I can see that you are feeling…', 'I can hear how upset you are…' and 'I am so sorry that happened…'). ☐ Reinforce that it is OK to experience the feelings and emotions but there are OK and not OK ways of expressing them.

	☐ Apologise for something you did wrong or the way it was taken (e.g. 'I'm sorry that when I ……. it made you feel …….' and 'That was not my intention…..').
	☐ Thank the child for sharing their concerns, perspectives and difficulties.

DE-ESCALATION plan → **Talk about positive attitudes, choices and behaviours**

What?	Children need to develop positive attitudes, choices and behaviours.
Why?	Children need to develop positive attitudes, choices and behaviours to cope with frustration caused by inconveniences, stressors and problems that stand in the way of their goals.
How?	☐ Remind the child of your helping role. ☐ Discuss how frustrations provide an opportunity for us to grow by helping us develop positive attitudes, make better choices and learn appropriate ways of behaving.

DE-ESCALATION plan → **Identify appropriate alternative behaviour, Offer help, Note positives**

What?	Help the child to reflect on the incident, learn appropriate alternative ways of dealing with similar situations in the future and make amends to repair the relationship.
Why?	It is important to help the child understand the impact of their behaviour on themselves and others. By problem-solving together, it makes the process of talking about the incident less threatening.
How?	☐ Reinforce that you want the best outcome for the child and others. ☐ Discuss the incident individually or together as a group. ☐ Each child should have the opportunity to explain what happened in a sequential manner. ☐ Do not interrupt, discount or lecture the child as they are talking. ☐ Encourage the child and/or others take accountability for their role in the situation by taking ownership of their actions. ☐ Allow the child and/or others the time to explain the reasons why they took their actions. ☐ Make sure to encourage the child and/or others to appreciate the differences in perspective.

	☐ Encourage the child and/or others to reflect on what went well, what did not work well, and what behaviours need replacing.
	☐ Ask the child and/or others how the situation could be dealt with in the future. For example, 'I wonder what could be done next time if……; Can you think of another way…. or How else could we respond when ……?'
	☐ Brainstorm possible ways that everyone could respond in a similar situation in the future.
	☐ Listen to the suggestions.
	☐ Offer suggestions if appropriate for the child and/or others to consider.
	☐ Discuss the consequences of each possible suggestion.
	☐ Choose the most effective solution, i.e. appropriate alternative behaviours for next time, collaboratively.
	☐ Help the child apologise to others.
	☐ Talk to the child and/or others about the two choices they have to move forward from the incident– focus on revenge or forgive.
	☐ Talk to the child and/or others about the meaning of revenge and forgiveness. Revenge is the action of hurting or harming someone in response to an injury or wrong suffered at their hands. Forgiveness is releasing the need for revenge, releasing resentment and releasing negative thoughts about the situation and replacing it with something positive and loving.
	☐ Explain to the child and/or others the impact that forgiveness and unforgiveness have on the self. By forgiving the other person, place or thing, one experiences less anxiety, stress and hostility on the inside. One also has improved self-esteem and healthier relationships. However, when one is unforgiving, they become so consumed by the wrong that has happened they can't enjoy the present. They feel angry, bitter, anxious or depressed and this affects every experience they have.
	☐ Thank everyone for talking through the problem.
	☐ Remind everyone that they can come and talk anytime.
	☐ Set up a regular time to catch up with the child so that their progress can be monitored and any issues or concerns can be addressed in a timely manner.
	☐ Help everyone to return to an activity.

De-escalation Plan Form

Child name _____ Date _____

Recorder name/s _____

Triggers
Mild Escalation Stage
Moderate Escalation Stage
Extreme Escalation Stage
Recovery Stage

7. PREVENT STAGE

Once the Manage stage of the behaviour has been completed, the next stage is to prevent its recurrence.

The Prevent stage involves the team working through the checklist tasks listed:

Prevent Stage Checklist:

- Prevent plan – aims to detail strategies to minimise or avoid the triggers that contribute to the argumentative behaviours by providing the child with a supportive environment, activities and interactions, and by teaching the child skills for positive behaviour and managing emotions.

To develop the prevention plan for the child, discuss the strategies listed on the following pages with the team. Not all the strategies will suit every context or meet the child's particular needs, so select and edit them as appropriate. If recorded on paper, complete the *Prevent plan* form provided at the end of this section. . Alternatively, if using the Behaviour Help web-based app, start by selecting 'Prevent Escalation' and select the relevant items. Additionally, refer to the following behaviour-customised checklists and add selected items to the app.

Supportive activities → Activity participation

What?	Maintain flexible expectations of the child's level of participation from activity to activity based on their needs.
Why?	Activity participation demands need to be adjusted to match the child's emotional needs otherwise the child may exhibit argumentative behaviours for a variety of functions (e.g. escape/avoid activity and/or gain/obtain adult interaction). As the child gains a sense of control, competence and connection with the activity, the child's level of participation can be gradually increased.
How?	☐ Foster the perspective that success is not defined by the outcome but giving things a go by participating at any level. ☐ Be responsive to the child's emotional needs by being flexible in participation level expectations.

	☐ Select the level of participation in activities that they are finding challenging by targeting the level closest to where the child is at and can do quite successfully:
	○ Level 1 – Child engages in observer participation by not actively partaking in activity (e.g. not being asked any questions, not required to do any homework, assignments or tests).
	○ Level 2 – Child engages in partial participation by actively partaking in one or more steps/tasks within the activity (e.g. being asked 1-2 questions, offered a choice of what homework, assignments or tests they would like to do).
	○ Level 3 – Child engages in complete participation by actively partaking in the entire activity (e.g. asked questions, submitting all homework, assignments and tests).
	☐ Provide multiple opportunities to repeat and practise each level before moving to the next level.
	☐ Gradually increase child's level of participation in the task.

Supportive activities → Activity visuals, materials and resources

What?	Use a variety of activity visuals, materials and resources to enable the child to accomplish tasks successfully.
Why?	If a child perceives an activity as being too difficult, too easy, too demanding, too ambiguous or not meaningful, these triggers can contribute to the argumentative behaviour for a variety of functions (e.g. escape/avoid activity; gain/obtain adult interaction). To address these triggers, it is important to provide scaffolding. Scaffolding refers to the particular kind of help, assistance and techniques that enables a child to do a task which they cannot quite manage on their own and which brings them closer to a state of competence that will enable them to carry out other similar tasks independently in the future (Maybin, Mercer & Stierer, 1992).
	Visual scaffolding is the use of physical artefacts, visual strategies, graphic organisers, mind maps and visual media in conjunction with verbal speech. Visual scaffolding helps the child better understand the information, make connections, better express themselves, promotes self-learning, increases independence and decreases anxiety. This is especially useful when dealing with a child with difficulties in attention, communication and emotional regulation skills. Visuals allow the child access to the information at any time without having to depend on others to verbally remind them, but also replaces the demand being given by an adult which can sometimes add stress to a situation.

	By providing the activity materials it can help the child get on with participating in the activity instead of feeling frustrated or stalling because they have forgotten the material.
	Providing assistive technology i.e. any device, system or design that addresses the child's needs can enhance their capacity and motivation to perform tasks that might otherwise be difficult or impossible.
	By providing the necessary activity visuals, materials and assistive technology resources, transitions around the room can also be minimised. This will help reduce movement around the room, as being in close physical proximity with other children increases the chance of the child doing things that can annoy, disturb, upset or amuse others and increase the chance of the occurrence of argumentative behaviour.

How?	☐ Physical artefacts
	    o Models
	    o Real objects
	
	☐ Visual strategies
	    o Break card
	    o Daily schedule
	    o Task analysis
	    o Rules chart
	    o Materials checklist
	    o Instruction summary
	    o Reward system
	    o Free time activity choices
	    o Feelings chart
	    o Social story™
	    o Social script
	    o Comic strip conversations™
	    o Cause effect links
	
	☐ Graphic organisers
	    o Cluster chart
	    o Fact-opinion chart
	    o 5 W's chart
	    o KWL chart
	    o Persuasion map

- Sequence chart
- Story map
- Venn diagram
- Activity scaffold

☐ Mind maps
- Flow map
- Multi-flow map
- Brace map
- Tree map
- Circle maps
- Bubble maps
- Double bubble maps
- Bridge map

☐ Visual media
- Computer games
- Series
- Documentary
- Film
- Games
- Digital stories
- Apps

☐ Extra activity materials for the chid to borrow.

☐ Resources to reduce auditory distractions like noise cancelling headphones and ear plugs.

☐ Resources to help reduce visual distractions while working, such as workspace carrels, sparsely decorated areas and uncluttered activity areas.

☐ Resources to address child's sensory needs (e.g. sensory diet, sensory space and sensory tools), communication needs (e.g. visual strategies, taped lectures and communication devices), learning needs (e.g. modified work, multisensory materials and spelling tools), hearing needs (e.g. modifying acoustical environment, front row seating and hearing devices), physical needs (e.g. mobility accessible environment, adjustable workstation and alternative keyboards), vision needs (e.g. magnifiers, text to speech software and Brailler).

☐ Resources to create a digital or a physical portfolio containing a record of the

| | tasks the child has completed that the child can refer to build confidence in their abilities. |
| | ☐ Resources to create positive affirmation posters that can be used by the child to speak positive statements about themselves. |

Supportive activities → Activity design

What?	Create a balanced schedule with tailored activities that match the child's needs, abilities and preferences.
Why?	Creating such a schedule helps the child to learn effectively and progress. Children vary in their ability to cope with activity demands for a number of reasons e.g. ability to tolerate frustration, level of motivation, length of time they can pay attention, sense of competence to complete the activity, perceived meaningfulness and relevance of the activity. By creating a balanced schedule with tailored activities and reducing unstructured/idle time, opportunities are minimised for the child to go off task; which then requires some type of directive that creates the potential for a power struggle and frustration related to stopping a preferred activity. Also, providing the child with regular breaks helps them self-regulate, regain and maintain self-composure.
How?	☐ Create a balanced schedule for the child by tailoring activities to the child's abilities, interests and learning styles: 　o Alternate between difficult and easy activities. 　o Alternate between high and low interest tasks. 　o Alternate between passive and active tasks. 　o Insert highly stimulating activities in the daily schedule. 　o Ease transition from highly preferred activity to non-preferred activity by inserting a neutral or preferred activity in between. 　o Structure activities during unstructured times. 　o Insert a calming activity before and after stressful activities to help the child stay calm. 　o Insert activities in the daily schedule where the child has to help, give or do kind things for others. 　o Identify and allocate the child jobs or responsibilities which they can complete successfully. 　o Incorporate special interests and hobbies to increase motivation, engagement and participation in scheduled activities. 　o Incorporate a reward system to keep the child motivated throughout the day.

- Incorporate prescribed sensory diet into their schedule especially at times in the day when the argumentative behaviour is most likely to occur.
- Insert a calming activity before and after stressful activities to help the child remain calm.
- Include stress reduction breaks in the schedule at regular intervals to help the child release tension, relax their body and avoid becoming frustrated. Break activities include drinking water, physical and relaxation exercises, singing and doing minimal challenge tasks.
- Throughout the day encourage the child to do heavy work and movement activities (e.g. jumping, pushing, lifting, carrying, climbing) for their calming and organising effect.

☐ Tailor activities to increase engagement by adjusting:
- Difficulty of the activity so that there is a high rate of correct response.
- Activity length so that there is a high rate of positive engagement and avoidance of fatigue.
- Purpose and appropriateness of the task.
- Order of learning.
- Waiting periods.
- Pace and way instruction is delivered to the child.
- Amount of information provided at one time.
- Complexity of the task.
- Number of the items that the child is expected to learn.
- How the child can respond to the task.
- Time allowed for processing information, learning, task completion and testing.
- Amount of support provided to child.
- Number of opportunities provided to practise and develop the skill.
- Activity start and finish time.
- Time provided to *transition* to a *new* location or **activity**.

☐ Break activities down into small manageable steps/tasks/milestones.
☐ Use cooperative learning strategies to minimise competition in activities.
☐ Discuss the daily schedule with the child before commencing the day.
☐ Refer to the daily schedule at regular times throughout the day.

Supportive activities → Activity instruction

What?	Adapt the activity instruction method, reinforcement and management style to match the child's needs, abilities and preferences.
Why?	By making adaptations to the way instructions are provided, instruction related triggers that contribute to the argumentative behaviour can be minimised or avoided. This can result in increased compliance and enable the child to successfully participate in the activity from the beginning to the end.
How?	☐ Before commencing the activity ensure all the necessary visual aids, materials and resources are available. ☐ Remove items that are not being used to eliminate unnecessary distractions. ☐ Maintain pace and flow by minimising time taken to present information. ☐ Create rules with your child to help them understand behavioural expectations for each context (i.e. what behaviour is allowed and not allowed) along with the why behind these expectations. ☐ Review rules, expectations and consequences along with the why behind them before commencing the activity. ☐ Use a consistent pattern for starting activities. ☐ Gain the child's attention before giving instruction. ☐ Speak in a varied tone, pitch, volume and inflection to emphasise and add interest. ☐ Be aware of rate, length and complexity of provided information. ☐ Use a combination of visual, auditory and kinaesthetic (hands-on) activities to support verbal instruction. ☐ Organise instructions in sequence. ☐ Give one instruction at a time. ☐ Avoid instruction phrased as a yes/no question because the child could refuse. ☐ Avoid instruction phrased with an OK at the end because the child could refuse. ☐ Avoid instruction phrased as a command, as the child could feel challenged or threatened. ☐ Phrase instructions as polite one-step requests by ending them with please or thank you. ☐ Phrase instructions in 'first-then' format. ☐ Phrase instructions as request for help. ☐ Phrase instructions with two choices to guide the child's decision. ☐ Say 'please', 'thank you' and 'sorry', as this can make the instruction seem less demanding.

	☐ Offer choices where possible to reduce the opportunity for a power struggle. Use the model of choice diversity (Brown et al, 1993) to create and provide opportunities for choice making. For example, choice of materials/items used within an activity, choice between activities, choice to refuse participation in a certain part of the activity, choice of people to be included or excluded within an activity, choice of location of an activity, choice when an activity should occur and choice of when to end an activity. Briefly and clearly state the two choices.
	☐ Replace verbal demands with visual demands to depersonalise the instruction.
	☐ Depersonalise the instruction by explaining that the rule is the rule, and you can't change it, (e.g. department, administration or organisational policy).
	☐ Be selective about the number of questions, instructions and comments you give, as each demand can cause stress.
	☐ Embed a fun and humorous instructional approach if appropriate.
	☐ Deliver instruction and move away.
	☐ Provide time to process.
	☐ Provide extended time for compliance.
	☐ Keep talking to a minimum as the child engages in the activity.
	☐ Ask if the child needs assistance and offer help accordingly.
	☐ Encourage the child to identify and correct own errors.
	☐ Use private and discreet signals to remind the child to correct their behaviour refocus on activity.
	☐ Provide advance warning that the child will be called upon shortly.
	☐ Prepare and provide explanations for any changes.
	☐ Provide extra time and advance warnings to prepare the child for transitions by using countdowns and a finishing routine.
	☐ Have a consistent pattern for ending activities.
	☐ Ask the child to complete a behaviour reflection checklist to encourage self-evaluation, self-management and self-reinforcement skills.

Supportive interactions → Adult interaction

What?	Interact with the child in ways that demonstrate understanding, acceptance and responsiveness to the child's abilities, learning styles and preferences.
Why?	By consistently interacting in ways that are mindful of the child's needs, interaction related triggers that contribute to argumentative behaviour can be minimised or avoided. This will help the child feel valued, respected and supported, and lead to the establishment of trusting and healthy relationships.

How?	
	☐ Get agreement on green, orange and red situations that will be consistently used by all adults.
	☐ Establish consistency in behavioural reactions, expectations and management strategies between adults.
	☐ Get agreement on language that will be consistently used to give the child feedback.
	☐ Be approachable and friendly.
	☐ Demonstrate caring behaviour toward all children.
	☐ Show genuine interest in the child.
	☐ Build a relationship by getting to know the child's interests, personality and background.
	☐ Avoid making promises that are difficult to keep.
	☐ Model healthy ways of arguing and resolving the situation.
	☐ Communicate high but realistic expectations to the child that can be enforced consistently.
	☐ Do regular emotional check-ins to help child label and manage feelings and emotions in a healthy way.
	☐ Provide the child with frequent verbal and non-verbal positive reinforcement for engaging in positive behaviours.
	☐ Build understanding of relationship rights and responsibilities.
	☐ Praise the child for following the rules.
	☐ Provide the child with choice-making opportunities.
	☐ Be flexible in terms of placing demands on the child. For example, by the end of the week when the child is tired, they are more likely to escalate when being told 'No'.
	☐ Build the child's self-esteem, self-concept and self-confidence.
	☐ Strengthen the child's spirit, self-esteem and confidence by never shaming them.
	☐ Provide four positive encouragement statements to one corrective statement.
	☐ Acknowledge the child's positive contributions.
	☐ Avoid bringing attention to differences between the child and their peers.
	☐ Avoid situations or talking about topics with the child that can cause conflict.
	☐ Avoid being drawn into arguments, bargaining or excuses with the child.
	☐ Avoid taking what the child says or does personally.
	☐ Indicate what is agreed with, state position clearly and walk away.
	☐ Discuss things calmly, briefly and privately.
	☐ Before the child commences the task, discuss possible challenges they may experience before, during or after the task. Brainstorm with the child what they could

	say and do to proceed. Chat/child-centred/catch-up times should be scheduled into the week when the adult and child spend time together on a regular basis. It should be a distraction-free time where the child can choose what to talk about. Encourage the child to wait till the assigned time to chat about whatever they want to. Over time you can gradually reduce the number of scheduled meetings per week.

Supportive interactions → Peer interaction

What?	Support positive child–peer interaction so that relationships can be built and successful teamwork can be achieved.
Why?	Children can experience a range of social skill difficulties e.g. difficulties with understanding and using appropriate body language, difficulties with understanding the intentions of others and taking account of what other people don't know, resolving conflicts, difficulties or failure in forming, sustaining and understanding friendships. These difficulties negatively impact the child's ability to build relationships and work successfully with their peers. It can result in the child being rejected by their peers, experiencing low self-esteem and engaging in antisocial behaviour. While it is not possible to force friendships, it is possible to minimise or avoid peer related triggers that contribute to the argumentative behaviour and improve child-peer relationships.
How?	☐ Inform peers as appropriate of green, orange and red situations so that they support its implementation. ☐ Increase active supervision especially at times, places and with certain children that increase the likelihood of the argumentative behaviour, by moving closer – scanning –interacting –positive contact –positive reinforcement for appropriate behaviour or 'on the spot' teaching of appropriate alternative behaviour. ☐ Be mindful of how groups are organised, seated and number of children in an activity. ☐ Reduce access to instigating peers. ☐ Reduce access to peers that the child victimises. ☐ Intervene, redirect and provide peer mediation to manage disputes. ☐ Educate peers about the child's needs. ☐ Educate peers how to safely interact with the child. ☐ Educate peers on how to respond to the child who is trying to provoke them into an argument. Use a buddy system to help the child develop social relationships.

Supportive interactions → Teach skills

What?	Use direct, explicit and systematic teaching when the child is calm to provide the child with multiple opportunities to learn skills by: 1. discussing the importance of the skill and modelling the skill, 2. providing guided practise to coach the child on how to use the skill in staged situations that simulate the actual situation and 3. using the skill in a variety of contexts independently.
Why?	By helping the child learn the appropriate alternative behaviour to deal with the triggers/problems, the child's need to resort to argumentative behaviour can be minimised or avoided. Below are examples of some of the skills that can be targeted.
How?	☐ Build the child's understanding of argumentative behaviour by helping them: ☐ Identify situations that can give rise to an argument ☐ Categorise the situations into different sizes (i.e. not worth it, worth a little, worth a lot) Recognise healthy vs unhealthy ways of arguing. Healthy ways of arguing involve: 1. Categorising the importance of the disagreement (e.g. not worth it, worth a little or worth a lot). 2. Monitoring and managing one's emotional and behavioural response throughout the process to ensure one is speaking in a calm, confident and assertive manner. 3. Expressing one's needs and feelings in a respectful manner. 4. Thinking creatively to provide sufficient information/evidence to support reasons for one's view. 5. Listening to the other person's counter argument (opposing reasons) openly and fully. 6. Asking questions to clarify and understand the person's counter argument. 7. Thinking flexibly to allow oneself to see the situation in alternative ways to think about the validity and strength of the counter argument. 8. Thinking creatively to weigh the pros and cons of own thought process and counter argument. 9. If in agreement with the counter argument being adaptable, switch behavioural responses. 10. If still in disagreement, generating a rebuttal to explain why the counter argument is incomplete, illogical, weak or unsound. 11. Working with the other person to identify a mutually agreeable solution or 'agree to disagree' to resolve the disagreement.

12. Moving forward with the other person amicably.

- [ ] Unhealthy ways of arguing involve:
  1. Using a one-size-fits-all approach to view and respond to the importance of all disagreements.
  2. Expressing one's needs and feelings in an aggressive, passive or passive-aggressive manner instead of an assertive manner.
  3. Believing one is right and the other person is definitely wrong.
  4. Providing no or insufficient evidence and information to support one's reasons.
  5. Not listening to the other openly or fully, instead quickly making judgements, half listening and making assumptions which can lead to misinterpretation.
  6. Unwilling to consider, being inflexible and rigid so not changing one's view or response even though there is sufficient evidence.
  7. Having difficulty controlling one's emotions.
  8. Dominating the argument by shouting over, interrupting, belittling, discounting, criticising, giving hurtful and resentful reactions when the other person is speaking - to the point that the other person may not be able to take a turn to speak.
  9. Escalating quickly into challenging behaviours if the other person does not respond effectively. For example, becoming verbally aggressive (e.g. name calling, using threats, making unsubstantiated accusations, giving ultimatums and yelling), being physically aggressive (e.g. hitting, kicking and punching), ignoring the other person or crying and whining.
  10. Not seeing that the aim is to resolve the disagreement mutually or moving forward amicably with the other person. Instead, aiming to be the winner to demonstrate power/status/control, causing the child to say or do whatever it takes until the other person backs down.

- [ ] Develop understanding of consequences on themselves and others of healthy vs unhealthy ways of arguing.
- [ ] Teach the child healthy ways of arguing.
- [ ] Teach the child healthy ways of interpreting communications, actions and attitudes of others.
- [ ] Teach the child empathy so they can understand how their behaviour affects others in terms of their feelings, thoughts and actions towards the child.
- [ ] Teach the child how to be accountable for their decisions and actions.

- [ ] Teach the child how to move past and forgive stress- provoking situations that arise throughout the day. Guide the child to Forgive it- Drop it – Leave it – Let it go. In other words, help the child acknowledge their emotions about the situation and deal with the situation in a healthy manner; but once it's been dealt with, they need to move forward instead of getting stuck in their emotions and staying there.
- [ ] Teach skills for successful participation:
- [ ] Cognitive Skills
  - Attention skills (e.g. orient, focus, select, maintain and shift attention).
  - Memory skills (e.g. encode, store, retain and recall information).
  - Thinking skills (e.g. problem solve, make decisions, ask questions, construct plans, evaluate ideas, and create new ideas).
  - Executive functioning skills (e.g. plan, organise, sequence, monitor one's performance, utilise feedback, inhibit inappropriate response, being flexible, time management skills and self-regulation skills).

- [ ] Physical skills
  - Gross motor skills (e.g. crawl, sit, stand, walk, jump, climb, run, and roll).
  - Fine motor skills (e.g. eat, write, cut, construct, tie, paste, turn, open, squeeze, button, pour, paint and hold things).

- [ ] Communication skills
  - Receptive skills (e.g. understand routines, words, phrases, instructions, directions, questions and concepts).
  - Expressive skills (e.g. request/reject affection, objects, action, information, assistance, clarification, attention; making choices and sharing information).

- [ ] Social skills
  - Non-verbal social communication skills (e.g. eye contact, facial expression, gestures, body language, private vs. public behaviour, proximity, volume, and listening).
  - Verbal social communication skills (e.g. greet others, gain attention, asking for help, initiate/maintain/end conversations, assertive communication, share jokes, join a group, work co-operatively and make friends).
  - Play skills (e.g. sharing, turn-taking, waiting and engaging in different types of play).
  - Emotional regulation skills (i.e. identify, understand, regulate and work through one's own emotions; read, comprehend and empathise with emotional states in others).

	o Self-concept, self-esteem and self-efficacy skills.
	☐ Teach the child independence skills by targeting activity steps the child needs to learn and gradually fading prompts and supports. ☐ Teach about the growth mindset where frustrations, mistakes and failures are seen as opportunities to learn something new, gain a new skill and grow. ☐ Use behavioural contracts to help the child understand goal/expectations, consequences and rewards for compliance. ☐ Use tangible, edible, sensory, social and activity rewards to motivate the child to work towards their goal.

Supportive environments → Physical environment

What?	Purposefully arrange the environment in ways that are responsive to the needs of the child.
Why?	Providing an organised, predictable and distraction-free environment can help the child feel safe, in control and regulated. Providing the child with a calm down area that they can access regularly can help the child maintain their emotional control and/or regain emotional composure and not escalate.
How?	☐ Create a clutter free and organised environment by using labelled storage systems to store materials. ☐ Designate and label specific places for items to be placed. ☐ Divide the environment into activity specific areas. ☐ Label the activity specific areas. ☐ Create physical and/or visual boundaries to help the child know where each activity area begins and ends. ☐ Reduce visually distracting stimuli ☐ Reduce auditory stimuli. ☐ Set up the environment to provide maximum personal space for everyone. ☐ Allocate a calm down area.

Supportive environments → Positioning in environment

What?	Position the child in the environment in ways that are responsive to their needs.
Why?	Considered positioning of the child in the environment can minimise or avoid triggers that contribute to the argumentative behaviour by instead enabling them to focus, develop skills and stay on task.
How?	☐ Position the child near the front of the room (see or not see peers). ☐ Position the child in close proximity to adult for prompting, correction or reinforcement. ☐ Position the child next to peers who can ignore the child's mild escalation behaviours. ☐ Position the child next to peers who are good role models. ☐ Position the child away from noise generating areas. ☐ Position the child in an area with minimal visual distractions. ☐ Position the child in an area with minimal traffic flow. ☐ Position the child in an area with minimal distracting smells.

Supportive environments → Environmental routines

What?	Create and practice routines that help the child move around the environment in a smooth, efficient and organised manner.
Why?	Providing the child with multiple opportunities to practice the steps involved in transitioning between activities, people and locations can help the child learn how to carry them out as independently as possible.
How?	☐ Establish and practise routines for entering the environment. ☐ Establish and practise routines for getting ready for the activity. ☐ Establish and practise routines for using visuals. ☐ Establish and practise routines for collecting materials and resources. ☐ Establish and practise routines for moving around in the environment. ☐ Establish and practise routines for waiting. ☐ Establish and practise routines for leaving environment. ☐ Establish and practise routines for transitioning between locations. ☐ Establish and practise routines for transitioning between people.

Prevent Plan Form

Child name _____ Date _____

Recorder name/s _____

Strategies for supportive activities	
Strategies for supportive interactions	
Teach skills	
Strategies for supportive environments	

8. CONCLUSION

It is never too late to address argumentative behaviour, even if it has been occurring for a while. The journey of behavioural change is a cyclic, ongoing process that consists of three stages: Assess – Manage - Prevent. The first step of the journey is to Assess in order to understand the message (function) that the child is communicating through the argumentative behaviour, and then to develop a Management and Prevention plan.

Once the plan is implemented it is important to evaluate the effectiveness of the Manage and Prevent stages by repeating the Assess stage to measure the amount or type of progress that has been made. This can help you determine the effectiveness of the Manage and Prevent strategies and refine and adapt them to ultimately help the child reach their full potential.

Please remember while argumentative behaviour may not disappear overnight, with persistence, patience and perseverance, the child can gradually learn positive ways of behaving and managing their emotions.

9. REFERENCES

- American Psychiatric Association (2013). *Diagnostic and Statistical Manual of Mental Disorders (5th Ed.)*. Arlington, VA: American Psychiatric Publishing.

- British Columbia School Superintendents' Association (2011). *Supporting Students with Learning Disabilities: A Guide for Teachers.* Victoria, B.C.: Ministry of Education. Accessed on the 7th of October 2020 http://www.llbc.leg.bc.ca/public/pubdocs/bcdocs2011_2/498894/learning_disabilities_guide.pdf

- Brown, F., Belz, P., Corsi, L., Wenig, B. (1993). Choice diversity for people with severe disabilities. *Education and Training in Mental Retardation, 28,* 318–326.

- Department of Education Queensland (2011). *A guide for bus and taxi drivers of students with special needs.* State of Queensland: Department of Transport and Main Roads.

- Griffiths, D. M., & Gardner, W. I. (2002). The integrated biopsychosocial approach to challenging behaviours. In D. M. Griffiths, C. Stavrakaki, & J. Summers (Eds.), *Dual diagnosis: An introduction to the mental health needs of persons with developmental disabilities (pp. 81–114).* Sudbury, ON: Habilitative Mental Health Resource Network.

- Klass, C.S., Guskin, K.A., & Thomas, M. (1995). The early childhood program: Promoting children's development through and within relationships. Zero to Three 16, 9–17.

- Kuhn, D. & Udell, W. (2007). Coordinating own and other perspectives in argument. *Thinking & Reasoning, 13,* 90-104.

- Maybin, J., Mercer, N., & Stierer, B. (1992). Scaffolding learning in the classroom. In: Norman K (ed.) *Thinking Voices: The Work of the National Curriculum Project*. London: Hodder & Stoughton.

- Meysamie, A., Ghalehtaki, R., Ghazanfari, A., Daneshvarfard, M & Mohammadi, M. R. 2013. Prevalence and Associated Factors of Physical, Verbal and Relational Aggression among Iranian Preschoolers. *Iran Journal of Psychiatry, 8,* 138–144.

- Ohio Department of Education. (2002) *What Is a Functional Behavior Assessment? The "WHY" of a Behavior.* Columbus, OH.

- Prizant, B. M., Wetherby, A. M., Rubin, E., Laurent, A. C., & Rydell, P. J. (2006). *The SCERTS Model: A comprehensive educational approach for children with autism spectrum disorders: Volume II program planning & intervention.* Baltimore: Paul H. Brookes.

- Rainey, L., Elsman, E.B.M., Van Nispen, R.M.A., Van Leeuwen, L.M., & Van Rens, G.H.M.B. (2016). Comprehending the impact of low vision on the lives of children and adolescents: A qualitative approach. *Quality of Life Research, 25,* 2633 – 2643.

- Reisinger, L. (2014). Using a Bio-Psycho-Social Approach for Students With Severe Challenging Behaviours. *LEARNing Landscapes, 7,* 259–270.

- Schick, A. & Cierpka, M. (2016). Risk factors and prevention of aggressive behavior in children and adolescents. *Journal for Educational Research Online, 8,* 90–109.

APPENDIX:
BEHAVIOUR HELP WEB-BASED APP

Step by step guide to assessing-managing-preventing challenging behaviour

Who can use the Behaviour Help web-based app?

The Behaviour Help web-based app is a valuable tool for parents, childcare centres, preschools, primary/secondary schools, disability services, child and youth services ... anyone supporting individuals with emotional and behavioural difficulties.

What is unique about the Behaviour Help web-based app?

The Behaviour Help web-based app provides a bank of evidence-based, practical ideas, strategies and suggestions for the assessment, escalation profiling, management and prevention of emotional and behavioural difficulties. As a team of parents, caregivers, educators and professionals, you can select the ideas, strategies and suggestions that are appropriate and customise them to suit the child. Additionally, this printed guide contains many more ideas customised for the specific behavioural problem 'argumentative behaviour'. You can enter the relevant items, and even your own ideas, in the app. The software will put together a ready-to-print customised pdf behaviour Assessment, Intervention and Management Plan to help you transform the life of the child you support. This pdf document can then be shared with the team. The app allows you to update the documents as often as needed and digitally store all the behaviour support plans in the one place.

How many children can I use the Behaviour Help web-based app with?

You can create as many profiles on the app as you wish.

What devices can the Behaviour Help web-based app be used on?

Behaviour Help is a web-based app that can be used on your Mac or PC, or on a tablet.

How do I access the Behaviour Help web-based app?

Please visit www.behaviourhelp.com/app/#/signup.

ABOUT THE AUTHOR

Hi there,

I am Dolly Bhargava. I have completed a Bachelor of Applied Science in Speech Pathology from the University of Sydney, a Master of Special Education from the University of Newcastle, and Certificate IV in Training and Assessment.

Midway through my career I realised my passion was in supporting children, adolescents and adults with emotional and behavioural difficulties (EBD). So I started working extensively with individuals with EBD in a variety of contexts such as family homes, childcare centres, preschool, schools, respite care, post school options, employment services and corrective services.

I have created this series based on the practical wisdom I have gathered from working with individuals with EBD, their families, educators and professionals over the last 21 years. I hope this guide equips people with the knowledge, skills and tools to help your child learn positive ways of behaving and managing their emotions.

Dolly Bhargava

www.ingramcontent.com/pod-product-compliance
Lightning Source LLC
Chambersburg PA
CBHW080637230426

43663CB00016B/2904